Contents

Introduction

This is one of a series of books dealing with the rights of:

Private Tenants. Weekly, monthly or other periodic tenants, and tenants with leases of twenty-one years or less, together with lesser rights of occupation known as licences, in houses, flats or rooms, where the landlord is a private individual or company, or some other body whose tenants are not public tenants, and who does not otherwise fall within one of the following classes.

Public Tenants. Weekly, monthly or other periodic tenants, and tenants with leases of twenty-one years or less, together with lesser rights of occupation known as licences, in houses, flats or rooms, where the landlord is a local authority, registered housing association or trust, or a development corporation, and who does not fall within one of the following classes.

Owner Occupiers. Those who – with or without a mortgage – have a freehold interest in a house or flat, or a lease of more than twenty-one years.

Occupiers of Mobile Homes. Those living in caravans, houseboats or other moveable structures.

Tied Occupiers. Those who have accommodation – in houses, flats or rooms – from their employers, or otherwise on account of their employment.

Homeless Persons. Those who do not have a home in which they have a right to live together with those members of their families they would reasonably be expected to live with.

***

This series does not cover the rights of individuals who have been living somewhere as husband and wife (whether or not legally married) on a domestic breakdown. This book does not deal with the rights of tenants against each other, for example neighbouring tenants.

The law in Scotland and in Northern Ireland is different from the law in England and Wales which is described in this book; many of the details of the law are different, there are procedural differences, and in some cases there are actual differences in rights. However, much of the information contained in this book concerns rights which Parliament has given to tenants and other occupiers, and as a general rule when Parliament gives rights to occupiers in England and Wales it will seek to give the same rights to occupiers in Scotland, and sometimes also in Northern Ireland.

As an outline of what may well be available, this book may therefore still be of use to those in Scotland and Northern Ireland, although they should always be careful to check the position independently. Useful places to check are:

Shelter (Scotland),
65 Cockburn Street,
Edinburgh EH1 1BU.
Tel.: Edinburgh (031) 226 6347.

Shelter (Northern Ireland),
2 St John Street,
Omagh,
Co. Tyrone.
Tel.: Omagh (0662) 44985

***

The law on housing rights changes frequently. This is especially true of housing benefits (see Chapter 9), which may be expected to change every few months or so, at least as to amounts of benefit payable and often as to other details. This book describes the law as at 1 November 1984. You should always check if what it says is still correct: see Chapter 12 for where to get advice for housing benefits, see *Housing Benefits,* by Peter McGurk and Nick Raynsford, republished frequently by SHAC (The London Housing Aid Centre), 189a Old Brompton Road, London SW5 (tel.: 01-373 7276). Chapter 9 has relied heavily on that book.

***

This book is an outline of what rights are likely to be available to you, as a public tenant. For a number of reasons, it cannot tell you in precise detail the full extent of your rights in every situation. For one thing, what your rights are will always depend on the *facts* which apply to your housing circumstances, or which apply to a particular housing problem. There are, then, as many descriptions as there are different circumstances, and different problems – and that means that there are as many as there are individual readers.

For another thing, many of the rights described in this book have been granted by Act of Parliament. Even though an Act of Parliament may seem to say one thing, judges may interpret it in a way that seems to you, as a layperson, completely different. Then again, exactly what an individual contract of tenancy means, or what was agreed or what actually happened, may not be absolutely certain until a judge has considered it, and decided even if it seems clear enough to you.

It is, of course, quite wrong that people's housing rights should be at all uncertain, whether for these reasons, or as noted above because the law changes frequently, or because it seems to you complicated or not to add up to a lot of common sense. It is for these reasons that tenants and other occupiers are often unclear what rights they have, and often frightened to enforce what they think their rights may be, in case it results in them being turned out of their homes.

A related problem is that occupiers often do not know where to turn for advice or help (including legal help), and, when they do, sometimes feel that even the advisers can't tell them exactly what their position is.

The principal purpose of this series is to try and help people know what may be available to them, more than it is to tell them exactly what will or may happen in every given situation. The way the series works can best be described by referring to three stages.

The first stage for someone who has a problem, or who just wants to understand his or her situation, is to know that there is, or at the least that there may be, some right, or entitlement, or even a discretion they may be able to take advantage of, and which may benefit them. This series seeks to encourage that knowledge by describing in outline what is available to what class of occupier, in respect of the main problems: security of tenure, paying for housing and disrepair.

The second stage is to claim the benefit of that right, entitlement or discretion. Administrators (or landlords, or others) do not shout aloud about what they are able to do to help, or even what the law *obliges* them to do to help. It is necessary to ask, and so far as possible to ask with some degree of confidence and accuracy. The series seeks to take the reader far enough to ask, at least in commonplace circumstances; "Isn't it your responsibility to do this, or give me that? Surely, I don't have to leave, or pay that high a rent?" Often, just asking is enough to produce a solution.

Finally, the third stage is when you are still not getting what you want, or you are unsure of what your exact rights are: the landlord is trying to evict you, wants to raise your rent, won't repair, or the local authority will not help you by forcing the landlord to repair or giving you help with paying your rent, and so on. It is this stage which cannot be covered by this series, because it would require the description of every detail of the whole body of law or administrative provision governing each subject, and covering every possible situation.

It is at this stage that resort must be had to advice agencies or lawyers. The availability – often without cost – of advice could be a subject for a book like this in itself. In most areas, there are Citizens' Advice Bureaux, Housing Aid or Action Centres, community groups providing or organising legal or informed advice, and lawyers who will provide assistance free of charge or at little cost, under the legal aid scheme (see Chapter 12).

Even at this stage, however, this series hopes to help: partly by encouraging the reader to take advice; partly because even lawyers are themselves often not familiar enough with the problems of the people likely to be interested in the class of right or entitlement with which this series is concerned. They may need prodding, to find out or check up on whether "something can't be done".

The "client" (reader) who can open a discussion with an adviser with the proposition that there is "probably" or even just "possibly" something which is relevant – using this book to say what – stands a much better chance of securing appropriate advice or aid than the client who cannot.

* * *

Against this background, there are a few "golden rules" which anyone who wants to make sure he or she has the very best chance of getting the most out of the housing rights which are available, without jeopardising the home should follow:

1. Always seek advice at the earliest possible opportunity, both to check your exact position and your best tactics.

2. Always keep copies of letters and other documents which you fill in, send or receive. Show them to your adviser.

3. Always keep a note, written as soon as possible afterwards, of any conversations you have with your landlord, his or her agents or employees, or representatives of a local authority. Date it, sign it and keep it. Show it to your adviser.

4. Even if you seem to have the right to do so, do not withhold your rent against something you think you are entitled to, such as works of repair, compensation for damage to your belongings, or a lower rent. Go on paying while you take advice and if necessary obtain a court order which proves what you are entitled to do.

5. Never quit accommodation, for example because of a high rent, disrepair or even just because your landlord tells you to do so, unless you definitely have somewhere else you are certain you want to go to and that you are certain you will be able to live in. Always take advice before quitting.

6. Stand up for your rights. Just because you are your only witness, and/or there is nothing in writing, does not mean that what you say will be disbelieved. Just because it seems difficult to get what you want, don't forget that a little bit of effort trying to establish your rights can sometimes bring substantial housing gains. Don't assume that everyone else – whether a landlord, or the local authority – is right, or more right than you are, or telling you the truth. Always check by taking informed advice.

1: Becoming a Public Tenant

Do I want to become a public tenant?

Almost everyone who has, or plans, to go on renting their homes wants to get housing in the public sector, i.e. from one of the public landlords such as a local authority, housing association or similar body (see Chapter 2).

For many years now, properly controlled private rented accommodation has been uneconomic for landlords. They can charge only limited rents, but must comply with public requirements as to the condition of their housing. Security of tenure means that tenants can occupy for their lives, and their family can take over and occupy for their lives in turn.

Private landlords are of the view that no one really wants them to continue to operate. They are correct. They are an anachronism, and the sooner they disappear the better will housing conditions be for everyone. In the meantime, they may be considered in three classes.

There are those who still have accommodation they rent out, in a normal way. There are very few new normal private-sector lettings. The physical conditions are not good, and regardless of how much security of tenure you have, you still tend to feel vulnerable to a landlord whose only interest is in the money he or she can extract from you.

Then there are people who rent out parts of their own home. This is understandable, and conditions are likely to be much better than when the landlord does not live in the house. However, the tenants of resident landlords have very little security of tenure, and it is certainly inhibiting to rent accommodation from an owner who lives in the same house.

Finally, there are the landlords who descend on the remnants of the private sector, squeezing as much as possible out of property, regardless of condition, maximising the profit they can make out of other people's desperate housing need. They let out accommodation – to people who really want no more than a normal home – on various forms of insecure arrangement, such as shorthold lettings, holiday lettings and lettings where the landlord can choose whom you share with.

Regardless of physical conditions, these are not the circumstances in which anyone ought to have to live indefinitely, as a home: you ought not in this day and age to have to answer to someone who is motivated only by profit; nor ought your security to be anything other than permanent.

For the last half-century and more, private landlords have been gradually replaced, in two ways. First of all, more and more people can buy their own homes: in 1915, less than 10 per cent of the nation lived in homes they owned; today, it is close to 60 per cent. Secondly, the "public sector" has risen, unmotivated by profit, to provide housing, with the help of public funds, today for approximately 30 per cent of the country.

The best known of these public providers of subsidised housing are the local authorities. There are also the housing associations, with a long and honourable history of seeking to improve the housing conditions of those who cannot buy their own accommodation, or pay for luxury accommodation, which stretches back into the last century.

Public housing may either have been specially built for the public sector or may have been bought out of the private sector. Much of it is of a very high standard, although there have been some serious errors in design and construction of purpose-built public housing, out of which people are being gradually (even if all too gradually) moved.

Much of that which was bought out of the private sector is of a lower standard, as is much that was built at the beginnings of the public sector, but even these classes of property may already have been improved, or will, eventually (even if sometimes it seems, all too slowly) be improved.

Those whose homes are provided in the public sector may, accordingly, consider that they either are in better accommodation than in the private sector or that they will – or at least ought to – finally occupy better accommodation.

Where accommodation is substandard, there are pressures which may be put on the landlord, not confined to the individual legal remedies common to the private sector (see Chapter 10), but by way of concerted political action (see Chapter 11).

In addition, most public-sector tenants have security for life. Many have the right actually to purchase – or part-purchase – their homes, and otherwise there has recently been a considerable advance in the package of rights designed to protect them against unnecessary policies or unfair changes.

Even if they do not buy, in some circumstances they can carry out improvements and alterations to their own homes (see Chapter 10).

Throughout, they are dealing with landlords who are in some sense "publicly accountable", either directly, because the landlord is an elected local authority, or indirectly, because none of the public landlords can afford to attract continuing adverse publicity from the media.

The very purpose of public landlords is to serve their tenants, and this is undermined when tenant-dissatisfaction mounts to a point when the public itself starts to pay attention to it.

This is a very different way of life from that which is suffered by the tenants of private landlords, who seek no more than their rent, at the lowest possible expenditure on repairs or facilities, and who not only are not accountable to the public but for the most part are indifferent to public opinion.

I am not saying that life in the public sector is perfect, merely that when problems arise, they are sometimes easier to resolve, there are more "weapons" available to the public tenant, and – perhaps in a home above all – there is a markedly lower sensation of insecurity.

How do I find housing in the public sector?

The short answer is, with difficulty. The position until comparatively recently was that the public landlords could provide their accommodation more or less to whom they wanted, within the criteria they set for themselves.

Thus, many housing associations or trusts (see Chapter 2) were set up with the specific object of helping a particular type of individual, such as the disabled, an ethnic minority, widows or widowers, unmarried parents, etc. Nevertheless, *which* individual within the group was given housing depended on the association or trust's own "allocation system".

Other associations and trusts, and all local authorities and development corporations (see Chapter 2) do not cater only for a special class of individual. They cater generally for people who cannot afford to buy or cannot find private rented accommodation, and want to live in the public sector, and, again, they have had their own allocations systems.

Acquiring accommodation in the public sector is, with three qualifications, a matter of finding out what are the individual allocation systems peculiar to each public landlord. The three qualifications affect *only* local authorities, and in some cases only *some* of them.

(1) All local authorities except county councils (see Chapter 2) have long been obliged by law to afford a "reasonable preference" in the allocation of their accommodation to people occupying insanitary or overcrowded property, who have large families, or who are living in generally unsatisfactory accommodation.

What "reasonable preference" means, however, is a matter for each local authority. In practice, most local authorities operate "points systems", giving points for all of these matters as well as things like how many there are in the family, including children, how many people are sharing facilities, separate bedrooms, and perhaps such matters as employment or time in their area, and other features like family connections. A few authorities do not, in fact, have systems which match this minimal legal requirement, even today.

It must be said that save in a few relatively progressive areas you will be unlikely to get local authority accommodation if you are single and childless, without waiting a very long time indeed. You will stand a better chance with a housing association, but again, unless you have a special need (see above) you may have to wait a very long time, or not get anywhere at all.

(2) In addition to this class to whom authorities must provide a "reasonable preference", local authorities which are district councils or London Borough Councils are also *bound* to find accommodation – whether their own, or from somewhere else – for those who fall within duties set out in the Homeless Persons Act. This will be considered further, below, as the last subject in this chapter.

(3) Finally, circumstances in which a local authority may close or

otherwise prevent a house or part of a house from being used for human habitation are described in *The Private Tenant's Handbook*. In such circumstances, the authority will have to rehouse people living in the property.

How can I find out how landlords allocate?

Since 1980, the public landlords described in the next chapter have been obliged by law to set out their allocation policies and procedures in rules. A set of rules must be kept available for inspection, free of charge, by any member of the public, at the principal offices of the landlord or, in the case of a housing association or trust landlord, at the principal offices of a district council or London Borough in whose area the landlord operates. In the case of any of these landlords, any member of the public who actually wants a full set of the rules, not just to inspect them, is entitled to ask for a set and to be provided with a set, on payment of a reasonable fee. Furthermore, all these public landlords have to publish a *summary* of their rules, and provide a copy of the summary free of charge, to any member of the public who asks for one.

What should I do if I think I qualify but the landlord still will not give me a tenancy?

The first thing to do is to check that the landlord has properly recorded your details. A mistake may have been made, or there may have been a misunderstanding, or it may be that you were never asked about something you have found out from the rules or the summary is relevant. You are entitled, without charge, to see what the landlord has recorded that *you* have told it about your application. This does not mean everything recorded about you, for example the landlord's own observations or possibly what it has heard from someone else, such as a former landlord. But your landlord has to show you what it has put down as having been told it *by you*.

What if the landlord has got it wrong, and will not change my details?

It is fairly unlikely that a landlord will not correct your details, although if there is some doubt about whether or not you are telling the truth landlords are entitled to record what you have said on separate occasions. Otherwise, you can complain to a senior officer, a councillor, or in the case of a local authority the Ombudsman (see Chapter 12). If they still will not correct the details, you may be able to compel them to do so, by legal action, for which you will need advice and assistance (see Chapter 12).

What if they still will not provide me with somewhere, when I qualify under their rules?

In the case of a local authority (see Chapter 2), you can complain to a senior officer, a councillor or the Ombudsman, and if all else fails you may also be able to take legal action, for which you will need advice and assistance (see Chapter 12).

In the case of a housing association, you can complain to a senior officer, or a member of its management board, or to the Housing Corporation (see Chapter 12). In the case of a development corporation, you can complain to a senior officer, a member of the corporation's board or the Ombudsman (see Chapter 12).

What if the refusal to allocate to me is because of my sex or colour?

It is generally illegal to discriminate on the grounds of colour, race, nationality or ethnic or national origins, or of sex (i.e. female or male), either directly or indirectly, by introducing a condition into a letting which is not justifiable on some grounds other than race or sex, and which makes it more difficult for you, because of your race or sex, to take up the accommodation.

Thus, it will be illegal to refuse you accommodation, or to give you a lower priority, or to require that someone else guarantee your rent, in a way that would not be sought were it not for your race or sex, or to allocate rooms in one house to people of one race or sex and those in another house to people of another.

In the case of sex, however, the latter class of discrimination is legal if the accommodation includes shared dormitories or sleeping accommodation, or shared washing or sanitary facilities.

There are also exceptions for associations, which limit membership to people of a particular sex or race (defined *other* than by reference to colour; for example, national or ethnic grouping), and the purposes of which are to provide positive benefits to those who have traditionally suffered from discrimination, including housing.

It is also illegal for a landlord to refuse consent to a subletting (see Chapter 4), on racial or sexual grounds, to advertise in a discriminatory way, to instruct an employee or agent to discriminate illegally, or to put pressure on someone to discriminate.

Public landlords will not normally engage in any of these activities, although it is impossible to say that no discrimination occurs, either directly, or indirectly because a particular aspect of an allocations policy hurts one class or other of the population (for example, time in the area, or parents born in the area).

If you believe you have suffered from discrimination, there are two bodies – the Commission for Racial Equality and the Equal Opportunities Commission – which exist in order to try and enforce these laws. Anyone can take a complaint direct to the appropriate organisation, and each organisation maintains staff to investigate and pursue cases, either by informal means, or by pressing claims through the courts. Alternatively, you are entitled to take action by civil proceedings in the county court, on your own behalf.

Can I become a public tenant by taking over someone elses' tenancy?

This will only be possible in the circumstances described in Chapter 3. The circumstances include family transfers, succession on death, and exchanges. In other circumstances, you will not become a public tenant.

Do I have to pay to become a public tenant?

This is extremely unlikely. Some landlords may ask for a small deposit – perhaps for cost of key, or against arrears or against damage to furniture – but it is unusual. It is not illegal for public landlords to ask for a "premium" or "key money", but the only reason it has not been made illegal (as it has in the private sector) is because it is so uncommon.

Some landlords will require a tenant to clear off arrears on former property rented from them, or even very occasionally rented from another public landlord, before granting a new tenancy. Again, this is not illegal in most cases. However, if it is made a condition of an offer of accommodation to which you are otherwise entitled under the Homeless Persons Act (see next question) it will be illegal.

Public landlords can be harsh in this matter, by asking one person to clear the arrears of another – for instance, a spouse for the arrears or another spouse. With the same qualification about the Homeless Persons Act, this is not outright illegal, but it is unusual and of questionable validity. You should make it clear that you were not liable for the former rent, and complaints should be taken as high as possible.

In those circumstances where exchange of tenancy is permitted (see Chapter 3), no premium should be paid in connection with the exchange, either to you or by you. If this does happen, you may be vulnerable to an action for possession, and loss of the premises you have taken (see Chapter 7).

If you are asked for money in addition to the rent, and not as a deposit, by the employee of a public landlord, in order to be allocated somewhere, you should report the matter to the police. You may be tempted to take the tenancy first, and then complain. However, if that happens, not only may *you* also have committed an offence of bribery or corruption, but the landlord will probably evict you anyway.

When will I qualify under the Homeless Persons Act?

The Homeless Persons Act requires district councils and London Borough Councils to secure that accommodation is made available for certain people.

In outline, these people are: (a) the homeless or those threatened with homelessness, (b) with a priority need for accommodation, (c) who did not become homeless intentionally, and (d) responsibility for whom does not lie with another authority under the "local connection rules". All these terms are considered further below.

Even if you qualify, however, it does not mean authorities must provide their own accommodation, although they must afford a "reasonable preference" (see page 4) to those who are homeless, as they have to do for others in unsatisfactory housing conditions, in the allocation of their own properties. Instead, they can organise housing for you elsewhere, for example through another authority or a housing association, or theoretically even in the private sector. They could even help by giving you a mortgage with which to buy somewhere if you can afford the repayments.

In practice, however, most authorities discharge most of their duties under the Homeless Persons Act by providing somewhere of their own, though they may take a long time to do so, and leave you in unsatisfactory, temporary accommodation in the meantime.

If you qualify for assistance under the Homeless Persons Act the accommodation provided must be adequate to house you and anyone who might reasonably be expected to live with you (such as family, common-law relationships, someone you have lived with for a long time, someone you take care of or who takes care of you).

In addition, the housing must in other respects be suitable for your needs, as to location, size, etc. It is no good housing you on the tenth floor if you suffer from a physical disability. You should, however, be careful before refusing an offer, because the authority may not make you another. Always take advice (see Chapter 12) before saying no.

It can be quite difficult – or take a long time – to establish whether or not you will qualify for assistance, or for what type of assistance, under the Homeless Persons Act. If you are *already* homeless, and have what is called a "priority need for accommodation" (see below), the authority has to provide you with somewhere while it reaches its decision.

This does not, of course, mean the same sort of accommodation it must provide you with if it is going to find permanent rehousing for you. It may be, for example, in bed and breakfast accommodation. If authorities provide their own accommodation, you will not get all the rights of a normal tenant during this period (see Chapter 2).

A. Homelessness

The authority only has to help those who are homeless or threatened with homelessness. This means you have – or soon will have – nowhere to live.

You will have nowhere to live if: you are not a tenant somewhere; or enjoy some other right of occupation; or, if you are married your spouse does not have a tenancy or other right of occupation.

If you have been told to quit somewhere, you *may* be entitled to stay in occupation until a court orders you out. You will probably not be homeless until the court has actually told you to go, even though, for example, your notice to quit has expired.

If you are illegally evicted, from private accommodation, go straight to the local authority. It will either help you get back in, or else treat you as homeless.

If you are married, or have been living with someone as husband and wife, and are frightened to go back, because of violence or the threat of violence, you are already homeless, although the authority may help you to get an order to protect yourself, in which case you will cease to be homeless.

If you live in a mobile home, or on a boat, and have nowhere you can legally both put it, and live in it, you are homeless.

You are "threatened with homelessness" twenty-eight days before you are likely to become actually homeless. This is the earliest time when authorities have to consider you as a Homeless Persons Act case, rather than as a normal applicant. If you approach them when you are threatened with homelessness, their actual housing duties do not start until you become homeless in fact.

B. Priority Need

You have a priority need for accommodation if you, or someone you live with, has dependent children living with you, or who would be expected to live with you if it wasn't for the fact that you have nowhere to live. Thus, if the children are with relatives because of the homelessness, or even in social-work care, you are still in priority need; but if your children have been taken from you for another reason, you are not. Children are usually considered dependent if they are aged under 16, or if they are under 19 and still in full-time education.

You will also have a priority need if you or someone you live with, or might reasonably be expected to live with, is pregnant. Any degree of pregnancy counts – not just more than six, or seven, or eight months.

You are also in priority need if you, or someone you live with or who might reasonably be expected to live with you, is ''vulnerable'', i.e. less able to cope with finding their own accommodation, because of old age, mental illness or handicap, or physical disability, or some other special reason (or a combination of some or all of these features). Old age is normally taken as retirement age: 60 for women, 65 for men. Mental illness will be evidenced by a doctor, but subnormality not bad enough to need psychiatric treatment may qualify as mental handicap. The consequences of alcoholism or drug addiction on their own are unlikely to qualify, but taken together with other factors may do so.

Priority need also arises if your homelessness happens because of an emergency, such as fire or flood, even if you do not have dependent children, nor are elderly or handicapped, etc.

If you do not have a priority need, the authority does not have to provide you with housing, temporary or permanent.

C. Homeless Intentionally

This is the most controversial provision. It was intended to stop people giving up perfectly good accommodation, for example in the private sector, to get priority in public-sector accommodation. In practice, it has been used to avoid housing all sorts of people whose homelessness was not actually deliberate, just because it might be said that they could – if they had handled things in a different way – have avoided becoming homeless.

The description which follows is depressing. It is, however, still well worth applying, even if you think you *may* be treated as homeless intentionally, because attitudes vary considerably from one area to another, and what one authority considers intentional, another may well not. (See also page 15. How should I apply?)

To be treated as intentionally homeless, you have to have done something, or failed to do something, as a result of which you have lost accommodation which was available for you and anyone you might reasonably be expected to live with, and which it would have been reasonable for you to go on occupying.

If what you did, or failed to do, was because you did not know something relevant such as that you could get help with your rent (see Chapter 9), or that when you are told to leave by a landlord you do not have to go without a court order (see Chapter 7), you are not homeless intentionally.

But causing eviction by failing to pay rent can otherwise count, as can breaking a term of your tenancy, or doing something else which earns your eviction (see Chapter 7).

It will not be intentional homelessness, however, if what you lost was not available for everyone you might reasonably be expected to live with, either because you were not allowed to live there with them, or because it wasn't big enough.

It may be you have never had accommodation for yourself and your immediate family – for instance, your partner and children – in which case you ought not to be considered homeless intentionally for giving up where you have been living separately from them.

You also ought not to be considered homeless intentionally if it was not reasonable for you to go on living where you had been. Unfortunately, this is a matter the local authorities decide for themselves, so that even if *you* thought you couldn't reasonably be expected to have stayed, *they* might think differently. Thus, it will rarely be safe to quit accommodation just because it is of a bad standard. You should think instead of using rights to repair described in Chapter 10 (or, in relation to private tenants, in *The Private Tenant's Handbook*).

If you have a right to wait for an eviction order (see Chapter 7), you should not leave before a court tells you to, although in two cases former employees were held unintentionally homeless for not awaiting eviction orders from tied accommodation.

It is not just the last accommodation you occupied which the authority may take into account. If that accommodation was clearly of a temporary quality – for example, staying with family or friends, a holiday letting, a squat – it can go back to the loss of the last settled accommodation.

Once found "homeless intentionally", you are unlikely to be able to force the authority to rehouse you without an intervening period of settled accommodation, in other words without spending some time elsewhere under some normal arrangement, more or less adequate as to size and condition, and not merely for a short or limited time.

If you live with someone who has been found homeless intentionally, such as someone who has voluntarily and without good cause given up a job to which accommodation was tied, it is possible you will also be considered homeless intentionally. However, you are entitled to be considered in your own right, and if you can show you did everything possible to try and prevent him or her losing the accommodation, may succeed in your own application. Oddly enough, unless you have separated from the other person, he or she remains someone expected to reside with you, and therefore accommodation provided for you must be adequate for him or her as well.

If you have been told you are homeless intentionally, you should seek advice and assistance (see Chapter 12) without any delay whatsoever. Whether or not the authority's decision can be challenged, in law, may well depend on whether you get help quickly enough.

If you have been found homeless intentionally, the authority only has to provide you with accommodation for as long as it considers reasonable to give you a chance to find somewhere for yourself. This usually means four weeks.

During this period, you may be provided with temporary accommodation in, for example, bed and breakfast, or other property not owned by the authority. If the authority provides you with something it owns itself, so that it is your landlord for those few weeks, you do not acquire the usual rights of its tenants for this period (see Chapter 2).

D. Local Connection

If you are homeless, or threatened with homelessness, *and* in priority need, and did *not* become homeless intentionally, the authority *may* be able to pass your case to another authority. This will be so if: (a) you have *no* local connection with their area, *and* (b) you *do* have a local connection with that other area.

The authority *cannot* use this provision at all if you, or someone you can reasonably be expected to live with, runs the risk in the area it wants to send you back to, of domestic violence from someone you, or your partner, formerly lived with, or would be living with but for their violence. Domestic violence means actual (i.e. past) violence, or threats of (i.e. future) violence which are likely to be carried out.

A local connection means that you have a connection with an area because you live or have formerly lived there, or you have family living there, or you are employed there, or for some other special reason. There are extensive guidelines about what qualifies as "living in an area", and the family to be taken into account.

If the two authorities cannot agree who should house you, there is an arbitration system for deciding. While they go through this procedure, the authority you applied to will have to provide you with somewhere. This is likely to be temporary accommodation. If it provides you with property it owns, you will not get the usual rights of a tenant for this period (see Chapter 2).

You may think that the authority ought not to be using the local connection provisions at all, because you believe they do not apply, perhaps because you have a job in the area or for some other reason. In this case, you will need advice and assistance to challenge the decision to refer the matter to arbitration at all (see Chapter 12).

Seek such help as soon as you are told (as you will be, see below) that the authority plans to try and refer you elsewhere, because your rights may depend on how quickly you act. Do not await the outcome of the arbitration, in the hope it will leave you where you want to be. Instead, inform the authority you applied to that you disagree that you qualify for referral; if the matter goes to arbitration, notify the arbitrator in the same way; it will then be relatively safe to take part in the arbitration proceedings, in the hope that a strict legal challenge becomes unnecessary. In this way you have "reserved your options".

How should I apply as homeless?

You apply to the local *district* council (not county council) or to the London Borough Council for an area. Go to their Housing Aid Centre, or Homelessness Unit, or their Housing Department. You are entitled to apply to whichever of these councils you wish. The authority which you apply to has to make the key decisions: homelessness, priority need, above all – intentionality.

Because opinions can vary, if one authority decides you are *not* homeless intentionally, but that you *do* qualify for referral under the local connection provisions, there is little the authority you are sent back to can do about it, *even if you formerly applied to it and it held you homeless intentionally!*

If you fail at one authority, then, you can still apply to another, although you cannot reapply to the *same* authority unless there has been some change in circumstances, such as pregnancy creating a priority need, getting a job, or intervening settled accommodation.

If you are reading this before you find yourself homeless, and can realistically make a choice between two authorities – perhaps because you live in one and work in another, or live on a border – you would do well to find out what sort of attitudes prevail in each.

It would not be strictly true to say that Labour councils are sympathetic, while Tories aren't, but as a rule of thumb it works most of the time. On the other hand, if you have a clear-cut case, it is not fair on Labour councils to burden them with a housing obligation that may fall on a Tory council.

Either at the time you present yourself, or on a subsequent date, you will be formally interviewed. Some interviewing authorities are sympathetic, others are looking for ways to avoid having to house you. The latter may try to "lead" or "trap" you into an answer, basically to try and show that you became homeless intentionally.

If you can take advice before you apply, the advice agency (see Chapter 12) may be able to send someone with you. Or, if you can take a friend or someone you trust (such as a personnel officer, company welfare officer), it is best to do so, to have independent evidence later of what was said, and by whom.

The authorities are recommended by the government to allow someone to sit in with you in this way. If the officer will not let you, remind him or her politely that this is what the Homeless Persons Act Code of Guidance says, and try and do this much in front of your witness, even if you cannot then take your witness in with you during your interview.

Never lie to the authority, about your circumstances or how you came into them. It is a criminal offence to lie to try and get housing (for yourself, or indeed for someone else) under the Homeless Persons Act, and many authorities do not hesitate to prosecute.

You ought also to be warned, in simple language, of a further duty: to inform authorities of any change of circumstance relevant to your application, which occurs *prior* to their decision (see below). If you do not comply with this duty, *you commit a further offence*, which again many authorities do not hesitate to prosecute.

There will be no criminal offence if you were not given this warning. However, the officer may ask you to sign a written "warning", to prove you have been warned, and sometimes this is included in a bundle of documents (i.e. forms), which you are asked to sign, and it is easy not to notice. *Do not sign anything without reading it carefully.*

If you disagree with something that has been written down – for example, facts or opinion – *say so at once* and insist on it being changed. If the officer thinks you are "changing your story", and does not believe the alteration, there is still no excuse for him or her not to record "both" accounts, i.e. that in his or her view you said one thing first, and then another.

More likely, however, the officer will alter what has been said. At the time of your interview, or after, you are entitled to ask for a copy of what has been recorded, as having been told to the authority by you, as on any application: see above.

How will I know the authority's decision and the reasons for it?

Authorities are bound to give their decision, and the reasons for it, in writing. This includes a decision to refer you under the local connection rules.

The date of this decision is very important. First of all, it may affect what rights you have as a tenant (see Chapter 2). Secondly, it is important because if you wish to challenge an authority's decision, there are strict time-limits, which run from the date of the decision letter, and if you do not seek help quickly, you may be unable to do anything to change the decision.

Do not throw the letter away. Keep it, and take it with you if and when you seek advice (see Chapter 12).

Can the law be used to change a decision that I am not entitled to housing under the Homeless Persons Act?

Yes. However, the procedure is highly technical, and the grounds on which a court will interfere are limited. The courts acknowledge that opinions as to, for example, what is intentional homelessness can differ, and will not interfere unless an authority has gone outside the limits of valid opinion.

You will need advice and assistance (see Chapter 12). Note, however, that this will commonly not mean you have to go to court. Some authorities give out decisions, which refuse housing, in the hope that you will not take advice. Once you do, they prove willing to change their minds. This is, of course, quite improper procedure, but it happens.

What do I do if I cannot get somewhere from a local authority?

You can still try housing associations. You should also insist that the authority keeps your name on its waiting-list (which it is bound to do), because eventually you may get a place under normal allocations. Otherwise, you have no choice but to go, or to go back, to the private sector, and seek to find some settled accommodation (see page 13) for a period of time, such as in a house with a resident landlord. When that accommodation comes to an end, re-apply.

2: Types of Public Tenancy

Who is a public-sector tenant?

The term "public-sector tenant" is used in this book to cover a range of different people, in different types of accommodation, and under different rights of occupation, but with one main thing in common: they all rent from one of a group of "public sector landlords", who provide housing as a public service, not in order to make a profit out of it.

Who are the public-sector landlords?

The public-sector landlords – as that term is used in this book – are:

(1) Local authority
(2) Housing association or trust
(3) Development Corporation.

Note, however, that the term "housing association" has a wide meaning, and that such associations are sometimes concerned in activities which do not constitute "public-sector landlordism". These distinctions are described below, and when the term "housing association" is used in this book it does not apply to such bodies when acting in these additional ways.

What is a local authority?

A local authority is a body elected to carry out a wide range of functions in a particular area, often including providing housing.

There can be two local authorities in one area: a local (district) council, and a county council or, in London, a London Borough Council and the Greater London Council. Housing is usually provided by district councils, and London Borough Councils.

Local authorities provide subsidised housing, i.e. the rent you pay does not cover the cost of building or buying the property. The subsidy comes from public funds – government and the rates.

For the purposes of this book, the local authorities which qualify as public-sector landlords are: district councils, county councils, London Borough Councils, the Greater London Council, the

Common Council of the City of London, and the Council of the Isles of Scilly.

You may have accommodation from a local authority, under what is described as a "housing co-operative agreement". This is an agreement an authority may reach with a group of tenants, usually on an estate, allowing the association to handle some of the management functions.

What management functions they are allowed to exercise vary depending on the agreement itself. Your principal rights will not be affected. It may affect allocation, because the co-operative's committee may be allowed to choose new tenants. You will have learned this when you applied.

Even if, therefore, you live in such property, your landlord remains one of these public-sector landlords.

What is a housing association or trust?

Housing associations are run by "management committees", which come to be appointed in different ways, sometimes including representatives elected by their tenants.

The difference between a housing association and a housing trust is not important here (and will be referred to in the context of particular rights, elsewhere in this book). The people running a housing trust will be called trustees. In this book, I shall use the term housing association to include both associations, and trusts.

Like local authorities, housing associations provide subsidised housing, i.e. with the help of public funds (in their case mainly from central government, although they can also get funds from local authorities). Because housing associations are not run by publicly elected officials, there have to be controls on them to make sure they are suitable to handle public funds.

To ensure this is so, housing associations which want to receive public funds have to be "registered" with a central body known as the Housing Corporation. Almost all housing associations are now registered with the Corporation. If you are not sure if your landlord is registered, you can always find out (see Chapter 12).

If your landlord association is not registered with the Housing Corporation, then you are not in the public sector, and the landlord is like any other private landlord (see *The Private Tenant's Handbook*).

In the rest of this book, when I speak of a housing association, I mean not only both association and trust but an association or trust which is registered with the Housing Corporation.

However, I do *not* include housing associations, when they act in the performance of a private function, known as the grant of "assured tenancies". These are tenancies of relatively new property, construction of which started after 8 August 1980.

Assured tenancies are mainly aimed at the private sector, but a housing association, too, can seek and obtain approval (from the Secretary of State for the Environment) to grant them, although very few associations are in fact involved with assured tenancies at all. You will *not* have an assured tenancy if, at any time since the property was built, the premises have been occupied *other* than under an assured tenancy. In practice, you will always be told by the landlord that your tenancy is assured, rather than secure.

The rights of assured tenants are the rights of *business* tenants, "modified" to suit residences. They are described in greater detail in *The Private Tenant's Handbook* and will be ignored in the rest of this book.

The term "housing co-operative" may also appear in connection with housing associations. This type of co-operative is one where a group of people get together and form their own housing association. They elect a committee to run it, from among the membership, and the housing goes only to members. Members have to be people already living in the housing, or who want to live in its housing.

This sort of arrangement is sufficiently different from normal tenancy, that the co-operative is not included in the principal rules governing public-sector lettings, and so for the purposes of this book they are not considered public landlords. The rights of occupiers are determined by the individual, co-operative agreement.

What is a development corporation?

In some areas, the government does not consider that *elected authorities ought to provide some public services, including housing.* For example, new towns are managed by appointed boards. In the same way, urban development areas, specially chosen as such by the government, have government-appointed boards of management.

These bodies are known as development corporations. This term is also used to include the Commission for the New Towns, which is the central agency for local new town development boards, and the Development Board for Rural Wales. They are, if you like, appointed instead of elected local authorities, but otherwise there are many similarities, including that the housing they provide will be subsidised.

What about other "public-sounding" landlords?

There are other "public-sounding" landlords. Government departments occasionally own housing, perhaps on land they have bought for other purposes, perhaps for a caretaker or other employee to live in. The Crown, too, owns considerable rented residential accommodation.

In the case of Crown property, this may be under the management of an agency known as the Crown Estates Commissioners, in which case tenants are treated as fully protected *private* tenants (see *The Private Tenant's Handbook)*. Otherwise, their tenants, and those of government departments, are wholly without protection.

Then there are bodies such as the Church Commissioners, the British Museum, or the nationalised industries. Again, these are all treated as private landlords: see *The Private Tenant's Handbook.*

Does everyone who rents from a public-sector landlord have the same rights?

No. Excluding those described (as not to be dealt with in this book,) in relation to housing associations (see page 20), there are two main classes of public-sector occupier.

They are: those who have security of tenure, who are called "secure tenants"; and those who do not. If you have a perfectly normal renting arrangement from a public landlord, you will be a secure tenant; if you have an arrangement that is somehow "different", you may not be.

You are likely to know if you were provided with housing other than under a normal lettings system. If you do not know, you can always ask your own landlord: "Am I a secure tenant?" If the landlord says that you are, you almost certainly will be; if the landlord says that you are not, it is well worth making sure, because it have a much greater interest in *denying* your security than in *admitting* it.

Is every occupier a tenant?

No. Some rights of occupation are known as "licences". The term "licence" means "permission", and in the housing context means a permission to use or occupy housing, not as much or as formal as "tenancy", which is the traditional arrangement under which one person occupies housing belonging to another.

In the private sector, the distinction between tenancy and licence is of considerable importance. It is not important in the public sector. On occasion, some right may turn on this distinction, and I will identify this in its own context. In the main, though, the distinction has been abolished for most practical purposes and replaced with the distinctions described below.

Where I refer in this book, then, to "tenancy", I include "licence", *unless* I say otherwise. If you have been given a document which says that you are a licensee, you may treat it as if you were a tenant, save in these particular cases I shall refer to as we come to them.

This is of particular importance in relation to the main question considered in this chapter, below: whether or not you have a *secure* right of occupation. If you are a trespasser, however, i.e. a squatter (see page 31), you will *not* enjoy a secure – or indeed any – *right* of occupation (because the meaning of trespass is that there is no *right* as such).

Am I a secure tenant?

If you rent from a public sector landlord, you will probably be a secure tenant (or, of course, licensee – see last answer: all references to tenancy include licence, except where otherwise stated).

You will not be a secure tenant if you fall into any of the following classes (or if your arrangement is one of those described as excluded, in relation to housing associations – above).

A. Personal Use

(1) You do not use the place as your main or only home. If you are

one of joint tenants (see page 32), it is only necessary that one of you go on using the place as your main or only home.

If you are fortunate enough to be able to do so, you might have bought a place to retire to. You may visit it, for example, at weekends, or for your holidays. Alternatively, you may be able to have a holiday home somewhere. This sort of additional housing would not prevent you being a secure tenant in your "main" home.

To give another example, you may have an elderly relative, who needs looking after for so much of the time that you might be said to be "almost" living there, or living there "part-time". Again, this will not stop you being a secure tenant in your "main" home.

You will only not be a secure tenant if the place you rent from the public landlord is your subsidiary home, or if it is impossible to say which is your main home, i.e. if both are used equally. The public-sector property must be "more" your home than anywhere else.

B. Almshouses and Hostel-type Arrangements

(2) If you live in property owned by an almshouse charity, and you are charged no more than the amount which, from time to time, the Charity Commissioners specify for that almshouse charity, you will not be a secure tenant.

(3) What you rent is not a conventional, self-contained home, for instance if it is in a hostel and you have to share a room with someone the landlord has chosen, and/or you do not have your own cooking facilities but have to share with others of the landlord's choosing.

This may happen if you have gone into a hostel from hospital, or from prison. Some public-sector landlords provide hostels for the single, or the elderly. Hostel rooms are sometimes shared, and they usually have common facilities, for cooking and for recreation.

Similarly, such arrangements are sometimes provided for the victims of domestic violence, or for young single mothers, or for the handicapped or disabled, those in need of psychiatric or personal support, or those with an addiction difficulty.

It matters not whether what is provided is in a purpose-built hostel, or in a house, or even in a flat used as a "mini-hostel". It may or may not involve residential support or caretaking staff. The crucial elements which mean that there will not be a secure tenancy are:

(a) You do not have your own room, but share with someone the landlord has chosen (even if, perhaps, you have been able to persuade the landlord to select someone you want to share with); and/or

(b) what is provided is not a self-contained home, but there are common rooms, such as for recreation, and/or shared cooking rooms or facilities.

In this type of case, you will not be a secure tenant.

C. Long Leases/Shared Ownership

(4) You have a long lease, for twenty-one years or more, from the landlord, or a lease which you have "bought" or "part-bought" from the landlord, under one of the rights which secure tenants enjoy, known generally as the "right to buy" (see Chapter 5); these types of arrangement are, or are close to, forms of owner-occupation, rather than tenancy.

D. Employment Arrangements

(5) You have been given somewhere to live by the landlord in order to be able to carry out your job better (because, for example, you need to be close, such as a caretaker), and your employer is either your own landlord, or a local authority or development corporation.

(6) You are a police officer and have been provided with rent-free accommodation for that reason.

(7) You work for the fire brigade, need to live close to your work and have been provided with accommodation for that reason.

E. Time-Limited Special Cases

(8) The property you live in is usually used for one of the employment arrangement cases (Class D, 4-6) has been used under one of them at some time during the three years before you were allowed to live there, and before you were given the tenancy you were told in writing by the landlord that this provision applies.

This provision only applies for three years in all, so that if you are left in occupation, without the landlord trying to get you out, for more than three years, you will simply have become a secure tenant.

(See note on Class E, below.)

Don't confuse the two three-year periods. If you were granted the tenancy almost three years after one of classes 4-6 last lived there, for three years, it will be almost six years since one of them did so before this provision ceases to operate.

On the other hand, if you were granted the right to live there immediately after the last of them did so, and after three years the landlord leaves you in occupation, so that you have more than three years' occupation of your own, the provision will have ceased to apply and you will have become secure, much less than six years after the last of them left.

The three questions are: (i) has one of them lived there in the last three years; (ii) did the landlord tell you this provision applied before giving you the tenancy; and (iii) have you been allowed to live there for more than three years yourself?

(9) If you are a homeless person, and apply to a local authority, that authority may have to help you (see Chapter 1). They may give you somewhere, or arrange for one of the other public-sector landlords to give you somewhere, while they find out about your case.

Or, they may find that you became what is known as "homeless intentionally", in which case they only have to give you somewhere for a short time. Or, they may argue that some other local authority has the responsibility for finding you permanent accommodation, but they provide you with somewhere while they and that other authority are deciding.

In any of these cases, you will not be a secure tenant for a period of one year, starting from when they tell you what their decision is. If they omit to tell you their decision, as they are required to do, it may be possible to prove when they ought to have done so, and claim security from a year after, but this will certainly need legal advice and assistance (see Chapter 12).

If after the year is up, the landlord leaves you in occupation, without trying to get you out, you will simply become a secure tenant. (See further note on Class E, below.)

(10) You will also not be a secure tenant if you were given somewhere under a special "job mobility" scheme. This arises when you are given somewhere to live in an area (meaning, the area of a

district council or London Borough Council) where you were not living immediately beforehand, and three *further* conditions are fulfilled.

First of all, you found a job in the area where you are now living, *or* in the area of an adjoining district council/London Borough Council, *before* you were given the tenancy.

Secondly, before you were given the tenancy, you were told in writing by the landlord that this provision would apply.

Thirdly, you needed temporary accommodation in order to take up your job, while looking for somewhere permanent.

This provision only lasts for one year. If at the end of it, the landlord leaves you in occupation, without trying to get you out, you will simply become a secure tenant. (See further note on Class E, below.)

(11) If you are a student, who attends a "designated course" at a university or other college of further education, you may not be a secure tenant. A "designated course" is one which has been listed by the government for this purpose.

You will not be a secure tenant in this circumstance, if two conditions are fulfilled. First of all, you were given the place to live in order to be able to attend the course. Secondly, before you were given it, you were told in writing by the landlord that this provision would apply.

The provision will continue to apply for up to six months after the course ends, or – if you change courses – your new course ends (provided the new course is also a designated course). If you never take up your course, or another designated course, the provision applies for only six months from the grant of the tenancy.

If you are allowed to stay on after whichever of these six-month periods applies, and the landlord does not try to get you out, you will simply become a secure tenant. (See further note on Class E, below.)

Note on Class E

In relation to each of these classes, the important point is that you are only not secure for a period of time. During that time you have a non-secure tenancy, and your rights as such will be discussed in different parts of this book. The crucial question is whether you have *become* a secure tenant, by being left in occupation longer than the provision permits.

One of the main differences will be how your right of occupation as a non-secure tenant can be brought to an end. We will see in Chapter 7 that there are special procedures for secure tenants, and "normal" procedures for non-secure tenants.

There are two main possibilities. You may have been told you can only stay for a period of time, at the beginning, in which case you will have a fixed-term tenancy (see below). Or, you may have a simple "periodic tenancy" (see below), i.e. from week to week or month to month.

(a) Fixed term. If the time given is more than the time described above, then you will have become a secure tenant before the end of your tenancy, and will be safe. This is likely only to happen by accident or mistake on the part of the landlord.

If the time given is the same as or less than the time described above, for being non-secure, then at the end you have to leave, although the landlord will not be able actually to evict you without an eviction order from a court. Getting an order may take the landlord some time. During that time, you may pay, and the landlord may accept, rent.

In such circumstances, you may want to say: "Well, I wasn't secure under the fixed-term arrangement, but now I'm paying rent, and the landlord is accepting rent, and it's outside the time-limit. Why shouldn't that be considered a secure tenancy, in its own right?"

You may well have a good point! It will all depend. If the landlord has simply not got around to evicting you, for a period, whether or not you have been warned that the landlord will eventually get round to evicting you, a court is likely to say that no new tenancy was *intended*, and that you have not acquired new rights.

There are no rules for what the court will consider means that a new arrangement was, or was not, intended. All the facts have to be taken into account. For example, if the landlord warns you in a letter that it will take action, and then leaves it a longish time, perhaps even as much as a year, the landlord may still be able to say no new arrangement was intended.

But if the landlord fails to warn you that it still wants you to go, and simply leaves you in occupation for a similar sort of period, taking rent, a court may well say: whatever individual officers or a local authority or a board of management, etc., may actually have wanted, they have acted *as if* you had a new arrangement, and it can be upheld.

On this sort of argument, you will certainly need advice and assistance (see Chapter 12).

(b) *Periodic.* The point is really the same, except that the landlord has to give you notice to bring your (non-secure) tenancy to an end. If the landlord fails to bring it to an end (see Chapter 7) before the time described in relation to each class has run out, you will have become secure.

If the landlord does bring the arrangement to an end, at or before the time described for each class, there still has to be a court order before you can be made to leave in fact, and again this may take the landlord some time.

Nonetheless, you are "on warning" that the landlord wants you out, and it is correspondingly harder to argue that there has been a new arrangement, even if rent is paid and accepted.

It is not, however, impossible. If nothing further happens for a longish period, again say a year or more, the *argument* is available to you that the arrangement must be considered a new one, and because it is not within the time, a secure one.

Whether or not you will succeed depends on all the circumstances, and again you will need advice and assistance to try and succeed in this (see Chapter 12).

F. Arrangements with Private Landlords

(12) Under special arrangements, private-property owners sometimes rent accommodation which can be used to live in, *to* a public-sector landlord, for the public-sector landlord to sublet to someone else. Where this happens, the sub-tenant does not become a secure tenant. This is, however, a comparatively rare arrangement. You are certainly likely to have been told about it when you were allowed into occupation.

(13) Sometimes, public-sector landlords provide housing to

private-sector tenants, while works are carried out on their homes. This may happen if the public-sector landlord has ordered a private-sector landlord to carry those works out, for the benefit of the tenant, but the works cannot be carried out "around the tenant's head".

This class of temporary arrangement is not a secure tenancy. Again, you will have been warned about this, and your consent will have been needed, before it happens.

G. Mixed Use

(14) If what you rent includes land for farming, within the Agricultural Holdings Act 1948 (which protects farmers), you will not be a secure tenant.

(15) If the premises you rent are licensed premises, permitting drinking on the premises, such as a pub or a club, or a restaurant, you will not be a secure tenant.

(16) If the premises you rent are partly for another business use, falling within the Landlord and Tenant Act 1954, Part 11 (which protects businesses,) you will not be a secure tenant.

H. Short-Life Property

(17) If the property you live in was acquired by the landlord in order to demolish it, or else to carry out major alterations to it, such as conversion of a house into two flats, or a building which has not been used for housing into houses or flats, you will not be secure.

A landlord would not normally let out this sort of property, which is known as "short-life property", to the normal class of tenant it caters for. It may, however, be years before the landlord can get around to the demolition or other alteration programme in question, perhaps because of public-spending cuts. In turn, this means that property not appropriate for normal lettings might be left empty.

There is, understandably, a lot of public disapproval about leaving property empty, for lengthy periods, until a works programme can take place, when there are many who are homeless. Often, empty property of this order will be squatted, by people without permission to be there at all, but who have nowhere else to live. Squatters are not, of course, themselves secure.

Public landlords do not want the public disapproval. Nor do they like it when squatters just move in and take over. It can often be very hard to get them out again.

What the public landlords sometimes do, therefore, is let such property, on "short-life licences", to people they would not otherwise house, such as single people without children, or families not on their waiting-lists and without an absolute right to housing (see Chapter 1).

Sometimes, public landlords will let such property to groups of people, often young and/or single, to occupy for a time. They may even use the property, on a short-term basis, and as temporary accommodation, for people they will eventually find permanent accommodation for.

In none of these cases will the arrangement be one of secure tenancy.

(18) Sometimes, when squatters have moved into premises of the sort just described, the landlord does not try to get them out at once, just for the sake of it, but "regularises" the arrangement and grants the squatter permission to stay for a while, perhaps until the property is needed. The property none the less remains scheduled for major works, and accordingly the arrangement falls within the last paragraph and is not secure.

Alternatively, the landlord may offer the squatter some other property to live in temporarily. If that property is also scheduled for demolition or major works, it will still be within the last class, and not secure.

On occasion, however, property squatted is not scheduled for such works, or the landlord moves the squatter on a temporary basis, into property not scheduled for such works, but put aside for some other use (not "merely" for a normal letting), rather than evict the squatter at once.

If you have squatted somewhere, and the landlord agrees to let you stay for a while, or to move somewhere else for a while, as part of the arrangement to bring your squatting without permission to an end, you will not get a secure tenancy, unless that is what is specifically offered or what you are offered is a perfectly normal letting, in a normal home.

What is a squatter?

A squatter is a trespasser, i.e. has no permission to be on premises. If you were given the landlord's permission to be on premises, then whether or not you are secure is governed by the answers given above. If you start as a squatter, and are then given permission to stay on the same premises or to go somewhere else for a time, see paragraph (18) of the last answer.

Permission may be from anyone who has the power to grant it, or who would seem objectively to have such power. If a telephonist answers "yes" to your question: "Is it all right to squat your block of empty flats?" no one would seriously think that amounted to proper permission. But if a housing officer is asked, and says, "You can stay there for a time," either he or she actually has the power to let you do so, or at any rate it is reasonable to think he or she does.

An outgoing tenant cannot give you permission, if the tenancy has come to an end or is to come to an end while you are there.

But if the tenancy is to continue, because neither landlord nor tenant has done anything to bring it to an end, then the person with authority to let you in *is* the tenant, not the landlord, and so you will have permission, and not be a squatter. Your position will be that of anyone else living with, or in the property of, a tenant (see below).

If I do not pay rent, can I be a secure tenant?

Yes. Whether or not rent is paid is *not* one of the circumstances described above as preventing a tenancy being secure. It is, however, uncommon in the extreme for no rent to be paid, *without* falling within one of those classes, because there is usually a reason why rent is not required, such as because your accommodation is related to your job, or because it is short-life property in such bad condition that rent couldn't even be charged for its temporary use.

What is a joint tenancy?

A joint tenancy is when two or more people are given a tenancy "jointly". The tenant is neither one nor the other, but both, or all, of you. There will only be a joint tenancy if the landlord has agreed that you should both or all be the tenants, as distinct from when the tenancy is given to one person, who brings someone else in to live with him or her (see below).

It is also not joint tenancy when the landlord chooses two or more people separately to share a room, or indeed even a flat or house, unless the landlord expressly states that you are to share as joint tenants.

Does it make any difference if there is a joint tenancy?

It makes no difference to whether or not the tenancy is a secure tenancy. There are certain advantages. For example, if there is a joint tenancy, and one of the joint tenants wants to go away for a time, so that he or she cannot be said to be using the premises as a home for that period (see above), the tenancy will still be secure.

There are differences where security is involved, especially if one of you wants to go and the other to stay (see Chapter 7). All of the joint tenants are liable for the rent and other charges, and for the other terms of the agreement.

What is my position if I am not a joint tenant but I live with a public tenant?

Leaving aside the problem of domestic breakdown, i.e. where people are living together as husband and wife, which is not covered in this book, if you are not a joint tenant but live with someone who is a public tenant, *you do not have a public landlord.*

You may be either a sub-tenant, or a "sharer" (which is a form of "licence", see above), but in either event your landlord is a private individual (the public tenant). Public tenants are allowed to have sub-tenants and other people living with them: (see Chapter 4). But your rights as against that person are the same rights as a private occupier: see *The Private Tenant's Handbook.*

What happens if my landlord changes?

The landlord in the public sector does not often change. It can happen, though – for example, when the Greater London Council's property was transferred to the London Boroughs, or when property owned by a new-town corporation passes to a local authority.

All changes of landlord will have needed government consent. It is not impossible that your landlord will become a private landlord, in which case you will become a private tenant, but it is highly unlikely.

More likely is that local authority property passes to a housing association. In such a case, since a housing association is a public landlord you will remain secure, but it will make a difference to how your rent is calculated (see Chapter 8).

Will I be secure if I take over someone else's tenancy?

You will not be secure if you take over someone else's tenancy if that tenancy was itself not secure. In some circumstances, it *is* possible to take over someone else's secure tenancy and become the secure tenant yourself: for example on death, or taking over a parent's tenancy, or even on an exchange. These possibilities are considered in Chapter 3.

What does fixed term tenancy mean?

Most public-sector tenancies are indefinite, from week to week, or from month to month. Occasionally, a tenancy is granted for a fixed period, i.e. you know how long you can have the property for. A fixed period can be for any period, from one month to hundreds of years, though for the purposes of this book long leases are considered a form of owner-occupation and are not included.

Fixed-term tenancies may be granted in relation to one of the circumstances in which you are not secure (see page 25). Otherwise, your position is much the same with a fixed-term tenancy as without, subject to minor differences, mainly concerning procedures, which will be discussed in context in other parts of this book.

What does periodic tenancy mean?

The normal public-sector letting is from week to week, or month to month, and is intended to last indefinitely. This is called a "periodic tenancy" to distinguish it from fixed-term tenancy (see above). The main meaning it has is that the tenancy will continue "from period to period", until properly brought to an end (see Chapter 7 as to how and when tenancies can be ended).

Will I have any rights as a non-secure tenant?

Yes. Your rights will be described in the following parts of this book, under each of the relevant headings.

Do all non-secure tenants have the same rights?

No. There can be differences in non-secure lettings. The differences will be described in the following parts of the book, in context. However, these differences will often depend on whether you are a non-secure *tenant*, or a non-secure *licensee* (see above).

Those in almshouses, hostel-type arrangements, provided with temporary accommodation because of homelessness, and in short-life property are likely to have licences rather than tenancies.

Students, or others in the "time-limited" class of non-secure letting *may* have only a licence, if what they have been provided with is not a "normal" property, i.e. one that would not normally have been brought into use, other than for this, or some other similar, special use.

If you have a non-secure *licence*, but *not* a non-secure *tenancy*, there is one case in which you will have additional rights. This only occurs if the landlord is a housing association, and *not* a local authority or development corporation.

If you have a licence from an association, *and* you have been given at least one room for your own, exclusive use (i.e. you do not have to share with someone of the landlord's choosing), *and* you pay for your right of occupation, *and* what you pay for includes use of furniture or other facilities or services (apart from cold water and lavatory), you will have what is known as a "restricted contract".

You will not have a restricted contract, however, if included in what you obtain for your payments are meals, and the value of the meals you get accounts for a significant part of the rent. There is no absolute rule as to what is significant, but below 15 per cent is usually treated as insignificant, above 20 per cent significant, and in between is a grey area which will be decided in each case.

The type of letting most likely to fall into this class, if the landlord is a housing association, is what was described in the main answer, on whether or not a letting is secure, as "hostel-type accommodation" paragraph (3).

If you have a restricted contract, you have rights which are really designed for the private sector, and are more fully described in *The Private Tenant's Handbook.* They may be summarised here as: (a) if you wish to do so, you may ask a Rent Tribunal to decide what rent you ought to be paying; and (b) if you are evicted, a court can give you up to three months' additional time in which to go.

3: Change of Tenant

Can the person who is the tenant change?

In some circumstances, the person who is the tenant can change.

Regardless of the *rights* – as the tenant or would-be tenant – to take over a public tenancy, which are described in this chapter, however, you should not forget that on occasion (although not commonly) in addition to these rights a landlord may simply *agree*, voluntarily, to someone taking over a tenancy. It is always better to *ask*, if in doubt, than to change the tenant and *later* find it may have been wrong.

Are the rights to change the tenant the same for secure and non-secure occupiers?

No. The position is very different indeed. Secure tenants have much greater rights to change the tenant. Their rights will be described first. The limited rights of non-secure tenants will be described at the end of the chapter.

Secure Tenants

1. Change of Tenant on Death

What happens if the secure tenant dies?

This is the most important provision. The law now allows someone to take over a secure tenancy if the secure tenant dies. The person who takes over is known as the "successor".

Priority is given to spouses. If the secure tenant dies, then the tenancy may be taken over by his or her spouse, providing that at the time of death the spouse was living in the property in question as his or her only or main home (see Chapter 2, for the meaning of this phrase).

If there is no spouse to succeed, then a member of the family who was living in the property as an only or main home at the time of the death of the tenant, *and* who had been doing so for a year beforehand, may take over the tenancy.

Note that in the case of a non-spouse successor, he or she must have been living in the property *with* the deceased tenant. A short period – for example in hospital before death – will not exclude succession for this reason.

The difference is because spouses may have separated, without divorce, before death, and the *tenant* may have moved out. In that case, his or her spouse can still succeed, because he or she was living in the house at the time of death, even though the tenant wasn't. But the law does not allow for a "separation" between the tenant and other members of his or her family, in which the *tenant* moves out, leaving the other member of the family in occupation. That is why other members of the family must not only have been living in the property but *with* the deceased tenant.

If the tenant wants to go, leaving other members of the family (not including a spouse) in occupation, the tenancy should be *transferred:* (see page 39, Transfer to Member of the Family).

Member of the family, for the purposes of succession on death, means parent, grandparent, child, grandchild, brother, sister, uncle, aunt, nephew or niece, including step- and half-relationships and relationships in law (i.e. relations by marriage), as full. Illegitimate children are treated as legitimate. Also included as a member of the family, but not as a spouse, is someone who has been living with the deceased as husband or wife, i.e. without legally being married.

The spouse (i.e. legally married) takes priority over everyone else, then, followed by a member of the family, including common-law spouse. If there is more than one person qualified as a member of the family, only one will succeed. Initially, they should try to agree. If they cannot agree, the landlord can decide.

If I succeed, can they move me?

If you have succeeded as a spouse, no. If you have succeeded as another member of the family (including common-law spouse), however, then the landlord *may* be able to move you.

The landlord can only try to move you if it considers that the size of the premises is more than you need, *and* it offers somewhere else that is suitable for you to live in, *and* a court both agrees that the place is now too big for you and that it is *reasonable* to make you move (see further, Chapter 7).

When deciding whether or not it is reasonable to make you move, the court will take into account – along with anything else that seems relevant – your age, how long you have lived there as your only or main home and whether you were giving the deceased tenant financial or other help before the death.

The landlord can only try to make you move if it serves the initial notice with which all proceedings against secure tenants begin (see Chapter 7) not *sooner* than six months after the death (so as not to add to natural distress) nor *later* than twelve months after the death (so as not to create a false impression of security).

What happens if one of joint tenants dies?

In this case, under the ordinary law of the land, the remaining joint tenant takes over as sole tenant. This is so even if the remaining joint tenant could not have succeeded under the rules described above; in other words, it does not matter about relationship.

In addition, "succession" by one joint tenant, by taking over under the ordinary law of the land, takes priority or precedence over the classes of successor described above.

How many times can succession take place?

Only once. Furthermore, no succession will be possible if the deceased was one of joint tenants and the other had died earlier, leaving him or her as sole tenant. Nor will there be any right to succeed if there has already been a "family transfer" of the order described below (not including transfers on divorce – also referred to, but separately, below).

What if the tenancy has been left by will?

It is very uncommon for a periodic tenancy to be left by will. The provisions described above will take precedence over a will of a periodic (see Chaper 1) tenancy. It is marginally less uncommon for a fixed-term (see Chapter 1) tenancy to be left by will. If it is, then the will determines who succeeds: only if the tenancy is taken over by a person who uses the premises as an only or main home will the tenancy remain secure.

2. Transfer to Member of the Family

Can a secure tenant transfer the tenancy to a member of the family, other than on death?

Yes, probably. The basic rule is that a secure tenancy *cannot* be transferred – known in law as *assignment* – unless on death (see above), in proceedings on matrimonial breakdown (see page 43), or under the right to exchange (see page 44).

In addition, however, a secure tenancy *might* be capable of being assigned *to a person who could have succeeded to the tenancy*, had the tenant died rather than assigned it, i.e. to a successor (see above).

This means that if a secure tenant wants to retire and move away, he or she should be able to pass the tenancy on, for example to a child who has been living with him or her at that time, and for the previous twelve months.

One can only say *should* be able to, because at this point we have to consider not only the general position but also the particular position under the contract of tenancy itself. This makes the detail quite complicated. Because the laws have been developed through decades – even centuries! – and (of course) not with public tenancies in mind, they do not make a lot of sense, which is another reason the position is difficult both to explain and to follow.

The best thing to do is to decide which option (below, A, B or C) applies to you, and work through it slowly, considering exactly what it says, ignoring what is irrelevant to *your* case and noting what *does* seem to apply to you.

You will find, at the end, that what you have "extracted" from this complicated description – i.e. what applies to you – is not, after all, so very difficult or lengthy to understand.

The tenancy agreement may say nothing about assignment. There is then said to be "no prohibition" on assignment. In most tenancies, however, there is a clause which states that the tenancy cannot be assigned.

It may do this in one of two ways. It may say simply that it cannot be assigned. This is called an "absolute prohibition". Or, it may say that it cannot be assigned without the permission of the landlord. This is called a "qualified prohibition".

In order to establish whether a family-transfer is possible, it is necessary to consider these differences.

Option A. No Prohibition

If there is no prohibition on assignment, the family-transfer can take place, without the consent of the landlord. However, the assignment must be "valid", which means either that it is carried out by "deed", i.e. a signed and sealed document, or else that there is other strong evidence that the transfer has been agreed and has taken place.

As we are dealing here with perfectly lawful assignments, the landlord may *in writing* acknowledge your right to assign, and that the member of your family has taken over and is now the secure tenant.

Otherwise, the member of your family will be much safer if advice is sought about the best way to carry the assignment through: (see Chapter 12).

Option B. Absolute Prohibition

If the clause says that the tenancy cannot be assigned *at all*, then any change of tenant without the permission of the landlord may lead you – and the member of your family who has taken over – into difficulties. You can always ask the landlord for permission, and an exception may be made.

Otherwise, your contract of tenancy says that you cannot carry through the assignment. If you do so, what the problems are depends on how you do it.

If you simply quit and leave the member of your family to take over, it will be very hard to show that a *valid* assignment (see above, under No Prohibition) has taken place at all. It may be possible, but it will certainly be difficult. You will be far better off to have the assignment carried out properly, i.e. by deed.

In this way, the landlord has to admit that the member of your family has become its tenant, even though the term of the tenancy prohibiting assignment has been broken.

The landlord can then claim possession of the premises from the new tenant, on the ground of breach of term of tenancy (see Chapter 7). The new tenant can in turn defend those proceedings, saying that although a term of the tenancy has been broken, it is still not reasonable to order him or her to leave (see Chapter 7). The matter will then be one for the judge.

If you do not carry the assignment through properly, however, the landlord can argue that the member of your family has never become its tenant *at all*: if there is no *valid* assignment, the transfer has been ineffective – it is as if you have done nothing.

This means that you are still the tenant. There is no claim against *you* for breach of tenancy, because though you *tried*, you have *failed* to do so. If you have stopped living in the premises, however, you will no longer be a *secure* tenant (see Chapters 2 and 7). This means that all security, and accordingly, the home, will have been lost.

The only exception would be if the landlord decided, or because of the way it acted towards the new "tenant", was treated by the law *as if* it had decided, to take the tenant on as its own tenant, in any event. This will be a rare occurrence, and advice and assistance (see Chapter 12) will be needed in order to convince a court that this has happened.

Option C. Qualified Prohibition

If the tenancy says that there can be no assignment without the landlord's consent, then whether or not the agreement expressly says so, that consent cannot unreasonably be withheld.

A landlord cannot be treated as having *withheld* consent unless consent has been *asked for*. Unless the tenant (i.e. the "old" tenant) has actually sought permission, any assignment will be as ineffective as if the clause prevented all assignments.

Do not, however, confuse "withholding" of consent and "refusal". If the landlord is asked, and fails to answer within a reasonable period (say, six weeks to two months), consent has been withheld, just as if there is an express refusal. The question then is whether the withholding of consent has been unreasonable.

As the assignment will be to a member of your family, it is not very likely that consent can reasonably be withheld. In the example of someone retiring and passing the tenancy on to a member of the family who has been living with him or her, a withholding will probably not be reasonable.

It is not, however, impossible. For example, a couple with children may be given a tenancy. A member of their family, perhaps without children, moves in with them. A year later, the couple want to move on. In such a case, it is likely to be reasonable to withhold consent, and the more so if there are any grounds for suspicion that they first took the tenancy with this or a similar end in mind.

Another way in which a landlord might argue that it is unreasonable to grant consent relates to the circumstances in which a successor tenant may be moved after the death of a secure tenant. These circumstances were described above, but do not apply on a family transfer.

If the premises will be too big for the member of the family, once the secure tenant has gone, the landlord could accordingly argue that the assignment ought not to take place. In this case, however, the landlord will probably not succeed, *unless* it is also offering somewhere else that is suitable, i.e. as it would have to do to force a move after the death of the secure tenant.

If consent is withheld, there are two courses of action open. One is to go ahead and carry out the assignment, leaving it to the landlord to bring action. On the action, defend saying that the consent was unreasonably withheld, and therefore that the assignment was permissible.

The other course is to seek a ruling from a court that the consent has unreasonably been withheld. This is, of course, the safest approach, and much to be recommended. (See Chapter 12 for advice and assistance.)

If consent was *not* sought, then of course it was not unreasonably *withheld*. If the assignment has taken place nonetheless (and is ''valid'', see above, under No Prohibition), there will have been a breach of the terms of the tenancy, and the landlord will be able to commence action against the new tenant (see Chapter 7; see also under Absolute Prohibition).

However, if it can be shown that *had* consent been sought, the landlord *could not* reasonably have withheld it, it will still be possible to argue that no order for possession should be made, i.e. because the failure to seek consent was merely ''technical'', and had no real consequences adverse to the landlord (see Chapter 7).

This argument will not be available if a valid assignment cannot be proved, because the member of your family will not have become the tenant; you will still be the tenant. In that case, the position will be the same as under Absolute Prohibition, above.

To be adequately effective, even if the assignment is permitted, or is thought to be permissible, it ought always, therefore, to be carried out "validly" (see above, under No Prohibition).

If the assignment cannot be brought within any of these provisions, the member of your family is only likely to succeed in claiming the secure tenancy if the landlord treats him or her, or is deemed to have treated him or her, as tenant (see above, under Absolute Prohibition).

Can I be moved if there is a family transfer?

No, not for this reason. The provision which applies on death does not apply in this case. You can only be evicted on the other grounds, described in Chapter 7.

Can there be a family transfer from joint tenants?

Yes, if both or all the joint tenants agree, and the person to whom the tenancy is to be transferred could qualify as a successor of at least one of them – for example, the child of joint tenant parents.

3. Transfer on Domestic Breakdown

What if there is a divorce?

This book is not generally concerned with domestic breakdown. None the less, it may be helpful to outline the position.

If there has been violence between the parties, the violent party can be excluded by a court for a period of time, while long-term rearrangements are made. This is so whether the parties are married or have simply been living together as husband and wife. This will not, however, amount to a transfer of tenancy: it is a temporary rearrangement.

If the parties are actually (i.e. legally) married, then whether or not there has been violence, one partner can exclude the other, pending a divorce, if a court thinks it necessary, but only by court proceedings. This is also a temporary arrangement, not amounting to transfer of tenancy.

If there is a divorce, then a court can order the transfer of a secure tenancy, whether or not there is a prohibition on assignment. A transfer can be from one tenant to another, or from joint tenants to just one of them (for instance, from husband and wife as joint tenants, to wife as sole tenant). You have to apply for a transfer order, but you can do this at any time, even after divorce.

If the tenancy is taken away from a person who was already a *successor* (see page 36), the person to whom it is transferred will also be considered a successor.

Can I be moved after a court orders the tenancy to be transferred to me, during divorce proceedings?

No. The provisions governing moves after the death of a secure tenant (see page 37) do not apply following transfer on divorce, and only the other grounds for possession considered in Chapter 7 will apply.

4. Exchange of Secure Tenancy

When can I exchange my secure tenancy?

The "right to exchange" is a very new right. It came into law late in 1984. The law makes it a term of every secure tenancy – regardless of what a written agreement or other document (see Chapter 6) may say – that you can assign your tenancy to another secure tenant.

To do this, you need the written permission of your landlord, but this permission cannot be withheld except on specified grounds. The grounds for refusal are considered below.

Whom can I exchange with?

You can exchange with someone else who is a secure tenant – *whether or not of the same landlord* – who has the written consent of his or her landlord to the exchange, which again cannot be refused except on the specified grounds.

It is not necessary that an exchange be a direct swap, or a two-way exchange. There could be a three-way exchange, or even more, provided everyone has the written consent of their landlord to the exchange, and provided, of course, that they are all secure tenants.

What are the grounds for refusing consent?

The grounds on which a landlord may refuse are:

(1) You or the person intended to come into your premises are subject to an order for possession, in which a date has been set for you or him or her to quit (see Chapter 7). You cannot use exchange to avoid eviction.

(2) Similarly, if possession proceedings have already been begun against you or the person intended to take over your premises, or a notice has been given that such proceedings are to commence (see Chapter 7), you can (and probably will) be refused consent to exchange.

This is only so, however, if the ground on which the eviction proceedings have been started are one of the first group of grounds (1-5A) described in Chapter 7, in relation to which the landlord has to satisfy the court that it is reasonable to make the order, and which grounds imply some tenant-default.

This ground for refusing consent also only applies if the notice that proceedings are to be commenced against you, or the proposed new occupier, is still in force (see Chapter 7).

(3) The landlord can refuse if your premises are much bigger than the proposed new occupier reasonably requires.

(4) Similarly, the landlord can refuse if your premises are not reasonably suitable for the proposed new occupier and family – for example, if they will be much too *small*.

(5) Some property attached to, or in the grounds of, non-housing buildings, such as schools, or situated in a cemetery, and which has been let in connection with a job. This class of property is not within the right to buy (see Chapter 5). An exchange can be refused.

(6) If the landlord is a charity, with specific objects, i.e. to cater for people with particular difficulties, or a housing association letting only to people with special needs, and the proposed new occupier is not within that class of person, the exchange can be refused.

(7) If a property has special features making it suitable for

occupation by a physically disabled person (see Chapter 5), and if the proposed new occupier moved in there would be no such person living there, the exchange may be refused.

(8) If the accommodation is in a group of ''sheltered'' units, for which a social service or special facility is provided (such as for the elderly or the mentally handicapped), and if the proposed new occupier moved in there would be no such person living there, the exchange may be refused.

What happens if the landlord does not answer?

If the landlord has not replied within forty-two days, it cannot refuse consent on any of the grounds described above.

However, this does not mean that you have consent. Although the landlord cannot normally add a condition to consent, there is one circumstance, described below, in which it can do so. The landlord still has the right to add such a condition.

It follows that, unlike a situation where consent has been unreasonably withheld (see above), it is never appropriate simply to go ahead with the exchange, because there may well be technical difficulties which follow which *could* lead to the loss of one (or both) of the properties in question.

Instead, apply to a court for an order requiring the landlord to answer, or for a ruling that you are entitled to exchange. (For advice and assistance see Chapter 12.)

Can the landlord consent subject to conditions?

Only in one case: if you are in arrears with your rent, or you have broken another term of your tenancy, the landlord can grant consent conditional on your paying off the arrears, or remedying the breach of your tenancy (for example, evicting an unlawful sub-tenant, see Chapter 4; or, remedying damage to the premises, see Chapter 7).

If any other condition is attached, you may simply ignore it and need not even get a court to rule that it is inapplicable.

Should I pay, or accept money, on an exchange?

Never. If you take over a tenancy under an exchange and money was paid by or to you on the exchange, the landlord can seek an eviction order against you. (See Chapter 7. The court has to consider it reasonable to make the order, even if a money payment is proved.)

This is so even on a three-way transaction. For example, you pay Tenant A to let Tenant B move into his house, you move into Tenant B's house, and Tenant A moves into yours. You are now the tenant of Tenant B's house, but did not make a payment to Tenant B. You have still offended this rule.

The rule is also offended if you do not pay, but you accept money on an exchange, even if you do not ask for it.

Furthermore, if you have taken over the tenancy under a family transfer, and the person you took over from offended the rule, then an order can still be made against *you*. This, however, is only so if the person you took over from is (a) a member of your family (see page 37, but includes a spouse) *and* (b) is still living in the house with you.

Can I exchange with a non-secure tenant?

No. Such an exchange could only happen with the full consent of your landlord and the other landlord, and would require to be in writing for the safety of all concerned. You should not do this without advice (see Chapter 12).

How do I find someone to exchange with?

Some landlords maintain an exchange register. There is also a National Tenants' Exchange Scheme, which produces lists of tenants wanting exchanges, and you can both register with it and find information out from it: P.O. Box 170, London SW1P 3PX.

5. Transfer without Exchange

Can I transfer without exchange?

The public landlords with which we are concerned in this book have to maintain rules for governing "moves", whether to other property they own or to the property of anyone else, which do not classify as exchanges (such as medical transfers).

The landlords have to keep the rules available, provide copies for a reasonable fee, and publish and provide free summaries of the rules, in the same way that they have to do for allocations (see

Chapter 1).

The provisions entitling you to see what the landlord has recorded as relevant to an application for transfer, are the same as those on an application for accommodation itself (see Chapter 1).

6. Temporary Transfer

What if I want to go away for a while, can I temporarily transfer my tenancy to someone else?

There is no such thing as a temporary assignment. In the next chapter we shall consider when you may share your accommodation with someone else. In the same circumstances as you can share, and in the same way, you can leave someone in occupation while you are absent for a while.

There is, however, one word of warning. So long as you are living in the premises, with or without a sharer, you will remain a secure tenant, i.e. it will remain your only or main home. If you leave your home for a long period, even if you leave a sharer in occupation, it may appear that you have quit, sufficiently that the property may no longer be described as your only or main home.

In that case, you will have ceased to be a secure tenant. This will not happen if you only go away for a short while, or if who you leave in occupation is a member of your family who normally lives with you and you intend to come back. It will not happen if you are a joint tenant, and the other joint tenant will still be living there.

You *will* lose your security, however, if you sublet (see Chapter 4) the whole of your premises, whether at one time or at different times until the whole of it has been sublet, and whether to one sub-tenant or to several until the whole is sublet.

You may also have difficulty, even if who you let in is only a lodger or licensee (see Chapter 4), if you also let out the whole of the premises, again whether or not at one time, and again whether to just one person or to several.

You are certainly likely to lose your security if you take all your belongings away with you – furniture, clothes, etc. If you are going to be away for a time, you must make sure that you leave physical signs that you still regard the place as your home, and that you can prove that it was always your intention to come back.

If you have good reason for going – for example, to look after an elderly relative who is sick – you may be able to get the landlord's formal "agreement" in writing, acknowledging that you have not "left".

Non-secure occupiers

Can the occupier change if the tenancy is not secure?

If the arrangement is one of *licence*, rather than *tenancy* (see Chapter 2), the occupier cannot change, because a licence is a *personal* right.

If the agreement is one of tenancy, it will depend on the terms of the tenancy. This is much the same in law as considered in relation to family transfers (see page 39), although the practical possibilities and consequences are different.

The different ways the matter may have been dealt with were described above: No Prohibition, Absolute Prohibition, and Qualified Prohibition (in which case consent cannot reasonably be withheld).

Option A. No Prohibition

If there is no prohibition on assignment, one tenant can transfer to another, without the consent of the landlord. However, the assignment must be "valid", which means either that it is carried out by "deed" – that is, a signed and sealed document, preferably drawn up by a lawyer for safety's sake – or else that there is other strong evidence that the transfer has been agreed and has taken place.

Option B. Absolute Prohibition

If there is an absolute prohibition, then any change of tenant without the permission of the landlord will be ineffective. This means that either the person trying to take over will never even become the tenant, or that the landlord will anyway be able to end the tenancy quickly (see Chapter 7).

The only exception would be if the landlord decided or, because of the way it acted towards the new "tenant," was treated by the law as *if* it had decided, to take the tenant on as its own tenant, in any event. This will be a rare occurrence, and advice and assistance (see Chapter 12) will be needed in order to convince a court that this has happened.

Option C. Qualified Prohibition

If there is a qualified prohibition, there is still a need to seek consent, even though it cannot unreasonably be withheld. If consent is sought and withheld (which is not the same as refusal – see page 41), you can either go ahead with the transfer and defend a later action, which is risky, or seek a court ruling before the transfer takes place.

This is, of course, the safest approach, but unless there are some kind of business premises involved (see Chapter 2), or a relatively long fixed term (again, see Chapter 2), it is unlikely to be worth going through with the assignment at all, because of the ease (see Chapter 7) with which the landlord can bring a non-secure tenancy to an end anyhow.

In most cases concerning non-secure tenancies, it is likely to be held reasonable to withhold consent. If, however, one can say *both* that the incoming tenant is a respectable and responsible person *and* that the change will make no difference to the landlord, or to the landlord's rights, it may well not be reasonable to withhold consent.

Even if the assignment is permitted, or is thought to be permissible, it ought to be carried out "validly", (see above under No Prohibition). If the assignment cannot be brought within these provisions, you will only be able to impose a new tenant on the landlord if the landlord treats him or her, or is deemed to have treated him or her, as tenant (see above, under Absolute Prohibition).

What if a non-secure tenant divorces?

The position is the same as with secure tenancies, *except* that a court can only order the transfer of a non-secure tenancy if there is *no* prohibition on assignment, or if there is a *qualified* prohibition, and the landlord consents (see above).

What happens on the death of a non-secure tenant?

There is no provision for succession in the way there is for secure tenants. If a non-secure tenant dies, the tenancy "passes" on the laws which govern other "property". If there is a will, the tenancy passes to the personal representatives under the will.

If there is no will, the property passes first through the court system, to the President of the Family Division of the High Court, and then to the personal representatives when they apply to administer the estate.

If the tenancy is fixed-term (Chapter 2) then, unless it contains a provision for it to come to an end on the death of the tenant, the next-of-kin who inherits can continue to benefit from it (subject, of course, to undertaking the liabilities, i.e. paying the rent).

If the tenancy is periodic, then it still has to be brought to an end in the "usual way" (see Chapter 7), i.e. notice to quit must be served by the landlord, on the personal representatives under a will or who have taken out letters of administration, or on the President of the Family Division, who has technically become the tenant.

This is important. Until the tenancy is brought to an end, the landlord is not entitled to repossess the premises. It follows that if someone has been living with the deceased tenant, whether or not a member of his or her family, the landlord will not be able to evict them without first ending the tenancy.

When so little security is available, even a gain of a few weeks or months while these procedures are followed may be important.

4: Sharing the Premises

Can I share the premises with whomever I want?

If you are a secure tenant, normally, yes. You can always share with anyone else identified as your joint tenant (see Chapter 1). You can share with any members of your family, for whose benefit you were given the tenancy. In addition, you have a right to take in "lodgers" and sub-tenants (see below), although in the latter case only with the consent of your landlord.

What you must not do, however, is allow the premises to become "illegally overcrowded". If you do so, you will commit a criminal offence, for which you can be prosecuted.

If illegal overcrowding occurs because the landlord gives you somewhere too small for the family it knows you have living with you, you are unlikely to be prosecuted; otherwise – for example, because you have sublet or taken in lodgers – it is not impossible.

To save you the risk of prosecution, then, what amounts to illegal overcrowding is described later in this chapter.

The rights of non-secure occupiers to share their premises are much fewer than those of secure tenants, although they too are bound by the overcrowding laws. Their rights are described at the end of this chapter.

Secure Tenants

1. Lodgers

What is the difference between a lodger and a subtenant?

The word "lodger" is not defined in law; it is closest to, and would probably be treated the same as, the word "licence" which was mentioned in Chapter 2.

A licence is a much less formal arrangement than tenancy (which includes sub-tenancy). If you provide meals for your lodger, or you let him or her share your kitchen or your living-room, or any other facilities apart from the bathroom, you will be considered to have taken in a lodger, not to have sublet.

Similarly, if the person you take in shares a room with a member of your family, or someone else *you* choose, he or she will be a lodger, not a sub-tenant.

Even if he or she has his or her own room, and you provide in it cooking facilities, such as a small stove, you may still be able to show that the arrangement is one of lodging, not sub-tenancy, if, for instance, the person was a friend of yours beforehand, or a relative, or a friend of a friend, or you were doing him or her a favour.

If, however, you separate off part of your property, perhaps the top floor, and let more than one room, without sharing anything other than the bathroom, this may well be seen as sub-tenancy. It may well also be seen as sub-tenancy if you allow someone else into occupation, or several people, while you go and stay somewhere else (see Chapter 3).

If you are in any doubt, you should seek advice (see Chapter 12) *before* you allow the arrangement to start.

When can I take in a lodger?

As a secure tenant, you may allow anyone you like, and as many as you like, to live as a lodger in your property, subject only to the laws against overcrowding (see page 57).

2. Sub-tenants

When can I sublet?

As a secure tenant, you can sublet *part* of your premises with the consent of your landlord (and, again, subject to the overcrowding laws: see below); you cannot sublet the whole of the premises.

As you can only sublet *part*, if you have sublet, for example, one floor and then want to sublet the rest (while you go and stay somewhere else), this will not be possible (and, in any event, you would run the serious risk of ceasing to be considered a secure tenant, for want of using the premises as your home: see Chapters 1 and 3).

How do I get consent to a subletting of part?

Ask for it, in writing. Keep a copy of the letter.

Can the landlord refuse consent?

Yes. It can only do so, however, if it is reasonable to refuse. It is likely to be reasonable to refuse if the subletting would lead to overcrowding. It is also likely to be reasonable to refuse if the landlord is proposing to carry out works on your property, which would affect the part of it you want to sublet.

It may also be reasonable to refuse consent if, for example, the landlord knows you are proposing to charge an exorbitant rent to the sub-tenant, or if you have sublet on a previous occasion and trouble resulted, with you or with your neighbours.

It will not be reasonable to refuse consent just because the landlord has a policy of doing so.

How will I know why the landlord has refused consent?

If you apply in writing, the landlord is obliged to give you a written statement of reasons. If it does not do so, seek advice (see Chapter 12), and if necessary a court will order the landlord to comply with this obligation.

What happens if the landlord does not answer?

If the landlord does not answer within a reasonable time (say, six-eight weeks, less if you have told the landlord that you have reasons for wanting to carry out the subletting quickly, such as because the proposed subtenant will soon be homeless), the law treats the landlord as having refused consent.

Can consent be given subject to a condition?

No. If the landlord seeks to attach a condition – for instance: only for six months, only on payment of your own arrears, only on you carrying out some works to your property – you may simply ignore the condition.

What do I do if the landlord refuses consent?

If the landlord refuses consent and you consider the refusal unreasonable, there are two courses of action open to you. The safest course is to go to court for an order declaring that the refusal was unreasonable, and that you are allowed to sublet (see Chapter 12).

Alternatively, you could simply go ahead and carry out the subletting, leaving it to the landlord to bring proceedings against you, on the basis that subletting without consent is a breach of your tenancy (see Chapter 7). You can then defend those proceedings on the same ground: that consent had unreasonably been refused and ought therefore to be treated as given.

The latter course is riskier than the former. Whichever course you take, however, when the matter comes to court it is for the landlord to prove that the refusal was reasonable, *not* for you to prove it was unreasonable.

If you leave it till the landlord brings proceedings against you, and the court decides that the refusal was *reasonable*, it may still not be appropriate to make an eviction order against you.

First of all, if the landlord knew you had gone ahead with the subletting, but did nothing about it for a lengthy period, it may be that it will be treated as having "waived" (i.e. abandoned its rights in relation to) the breach. In this case, you would not be treated as having broken a term of your tenancy.

Even if this is not upheld, it may still not be reasonable to make the order (see Chapter 7). At the worst, the court ought to give you an opportunity to rectify the breach in your tenancy by evicting the subtenant (unless, of course, this is not the first time; or there are other grounds against you – see Chapter 7).

What happens if I do not ask for consent before the subletting?

You can still ask for consent afterwards, and the position is just as if you had asked for consent before, including that, if you wish to do so, you can challenge a refusal in court, without waiting for the landlord to try and evict you.

You can do this at any time before a court hearing for eviction, in other words, even after the notice which the landlord has to serve, informing you that it is seeking possession (see Chapter 7), has been delivered to you.

If you have never asked for consent before the landlord brings the matter into court, you can *still* raise the issue. If you can show that – even though you never asked – it has made no difference, because the landlord could not reasonably have refused consent, the court ought not to make an order against you.

At the worst, the court ought to give you the opportunity to rectify the fault by evicting the sub-tenant (unless, again, this is not the first time; or, there are other grounds against you – see Chapter 7.)

Can I sublet the whole of my premises, even for a short time?

No. This will be in breach a term of your tenancy, and may well be regarded as having given up occupation of the premises as an only or main home (see Chapter 1), so that you have ceased to be a secure tenant.

3. Rights of Lodgers and Sub-tenants

What will the rights of my sub-tenant or lodger be?

Unfortunately, these would be very lengthy to describe. He or she is not a public tenant, because you are the landlord, and you are not one of the public landlords (see Chapter 2)! The answers will be found in *The Private Tenant's Handbook*, in relation to what are known as "restricted contracts".

However, *you* should never evict either a lodger or a sub-tenant without a court order allowing you to do so. If you evict without a court order, or indeed if you try and harass the lodger or sub-tenant to get him or her to leave, you will commit a criminal offence (see *The Private Tenant's Handbook*).

4. Overcrowding

How many people are allowed to live in the premises?

The answer is: as many as mean that the premises will not be illegally overcrowded.

What is overcrowding in law?

Premises are overcrowded when specified standards are offended. The standards apply to the "home": a house, or a flat, or a room – whatever it is that you have rented. The mere fact that there is overcrowding in law, however, does not *necessarily* mean that there is *illegal overcrowding*.

Illegal overcrowding only happens when there are *both* (a) overcrowding in law, *and* (b) that overcrowding is such that an offence is committed (see below).

The home will be overcrowded whenever there are so many people living in it that any two or more people of the opposite sex (of 10 years of age or more) and who are not living together as husband and wife (whether or not legally married) have to sleep in the same room.

This does not mean as little as it at first sounds, because it is not only bedrooms which are taken into account, but any "living-rooms", meaning *not only* a bedroom, and a living-room itself, *but also* a kitchen big enough to accommodate a bed. It follows that the test is not whether two or more people at least 10 years old and of the opposite sex (other than husband and wife) *are* sleeping in the same room, but whether, by counting "heads" and "rooms", they *have* to do so.

However, there is a maximum of two persons to any one living-room, and this only applies if a room measures at least 110 square feet. In smaller rooms the maximum numbers are: less than 50 square feet, no one to occupy; 50 – less than 70 square feet, half a person; 70 – less than 90 square feet, one person; 90 – less than 110 square feet, one and a half people.

Furthermore, where there are only two rooms in the home, there is a maximum of three people who may live in it; three rooms, five persons; four rooms, seven and a half persons; five rooms or more, ten persons plus two people for each room more than five (that means in six rooms, twelve people; seven rooms, fourteen people, and so on).

The references to "half" a person are not a joke: children up to the age of one year do not count all; those aged from one to (and including) nine years count as a half.

To work out if there is overcrowding, then, start with the simpler calculation: allocate the right number of people to the right number of rooms. If this suggests the premises are *not* overcrowded, check room sizes to see if as many people are allowed to occupy each of the rooms under the second calculation.

Thus, there may be five people living in a house with three living-rooms, but if when one of the rooms is measured it is found to be less than 70 square feet, in which case either a half or no person can occupy it, the maximum number of occupants allowed would be four, or four and a half.

There are, however, two circumstances when what appears to be overcrowding is *not* treated as such in law. First, permission may be sought and obtained from the local authority, for "licensed" overcrowding for a period of up to one year at a time. Only you (not a landlord) can apply for such permission, and the permission must state the number who are to be allowed to stay. Secondly, purely temporary overcrowding, caused by a visit from a member of your family, is disregarded.

Can I find out if my premises are overcrowded other than by working it out for myself?

Yes. Rent books (see Chapter 8) have to contain a summary of these overcrowding provisions, a note about the possibility of getting permission for overcrowding from the local authority (who may, of course, also be your landlord) *and*, most important of all, a statement of how many occupiers are permitted. You can ask the local authority to provide a written statement as to how many people are capable of living in a property without causing it to be overcrowded. This may be done at the beginning of occupation or at any time.

What happens if premises are overcrowded?

If you allow premises to become overcrowded in law, you will commit a criminal offence. No offence is committed, however, if the overcrowding has resulted from "natural growth".

(There is also an exemption for overcrowding related to when the provisions were first introduced, in 1935. This might apply if your family has been in occupation since that date, but as this will be a relatively rare circumstance, and the details are considerable, it will not be described here. If you are accused of overcrowding, and your family *has* lived in the same house since 1935, take advice – see Chapter 12.)

Returning to natural growth, this occurs when a child of the family reaches a relevant age (i.e. 1 or 10 years old – see above).

To secure the protection of the "natural growth" defence, though, either before the child reaches the relevant age or before any prosecution is instituted for illegal overcrowding, you have to have applied to the local authority (even if they *are* the landlord) for rehousing, and not have refused an offer of suitable accommodation from them.

Nor will the defence apply if you have the opportunity to reduce the overcrowding by asking a lodger, who is not a member of your a lodger to leave if it is reasonably practicable for the lodger to go, in all the circumstances, having particular regard to whether or not the lodger has anywhere else to move to.

An offer from the authority will only amount to suitable accommodation if you will be able to live in it without overcrowding *and* the authority certifies that the accommodation is suitable to your needs, as regards security of tenure, proximity to work, your financial means, and in other respects.

If the authority is offering its own accommodation, it must offer a property with at least two bedrooms (*not* "any" living room) for four people, three bedrooms for five, and four bedrooms for seven. These are higher standards than the overcrowding standards themselves.

If there is overcrowding, and the natural-growth exemption does not apply, however, then you will be committing an offence.

The local authority, is entitled to serve a written notice requesting information about occupation, and it is a further offence to fail to answer or to tell what is known to be an untruth in the answer.

The local authority, if it is not the landlord, may also serve a notice on the landlord, informing the landlord of the overcrowding, and if the landlord then fails to bring proceedings for your eviction, it too may be considered to have committed an offence.

Non-secure occupiers

What are the sharing rights of non-secure occupiers?

These depend on (a) the terms of the occupation agreement, and (b) the overcrowding laws (which apply in the same way to non-secure occupiers as to secure tenants).

What are the terms of the occupation agreement?

These will vary from agreement to agreement and it is, accordingly, impossible to describe them here. Furthermore, because the security of tenure of non-secure occupiers is so limited, there is little value in a detailed analysis of rights which can be brought so quickly to an end (see Chapter 7).

What can be said is of a general nature. First of all, the right of occupation may not prohibit sharing, whether by subletting or by taking in licensees or lodgers. In this case, you are entitled to share, subject to the overcrowding laws.

Secondly, it may prohibit either sharing or subletting, and whether of the whole or part of the premises, "absolutely". This is the same as an absolute prohibition on assignment (see Chapter 3).

If you break this term of the agreement, the landlord will be able to bring the right of occupation to an end, whether it is a periodic or fixed-term (see Chapter 2) right. You will only be able to defend yourself if you can prove that the landlord knew about the breach and went on accepting rent, doing nothing about the breach, for so long, that it may be said to have abandoned its claim of breach.

This will be of assistance if you have a fixed-term right, but see the note below on periodic rights, as to how effective resistance in that case will be in practice.

The agreement may also prohibit licensees or sub-tenants, without the consent of the landlord. There is a difference here between licences and tenancies: the law will imply into a *tenancy* that the landlord can only withhold consent reasonably, but will not imply this into a *licence*.

It follows that the landlord can withhold unreasonably, in the case of a licence, unless the written agreement actually says that it cannot do so.

The law on withholding of consent in relation to tenancies is similar to that concerning assignment (see Chapter 3), *not* that applicable to subletting by secure tenants (see above). (There are, of course, similarities; but it is differences that are important to rights.)

In outline, consent must be sought, and if not sought it cannot be said that the landlord has unreasonably withheld it. The landlord ought not to withhold consent if it will make no difference to its rights if someone else is brought in.

If consent is withheld – by failure to answer, or actual refusal – you can either seek consent from a court or wait for the landlord to bring proceedings and then defend. In the case of periodic agreements, this is unlikely to be of any use, because the landlord can bring the agreement to an end without reason, in any event (see below).

It may be valuable in the case of a fixed term, if there is still some time to run. Also in the case of a fixed term, and if the agreement is one of tenancy, even if you do not persuade the court that consent has been withheld unreasonably, it can give you what is called "relief" (let you stay in) on terms, such as that you evict the sub-tenant (or other sharer).

In the same case – fixed-term tenancy – the court could also give you relief if you failed to seek consent (so that you cannot say consent has been withheld) *and* you can show that a refusal would in any event have been unreasonable. Your breach (the failure to seek consent) would have been "technical", i.e. it would have had no real or serious effects adverse to the landlord.

Returning to periodic agreements, the point which must be made is that the landlord can always determine the agreement (by notice to quit – see Chapter 7), without giving any reason for doing so.

It follows that there may not be much point in defending yourself and proving you had not broken the tenancy, because if the landlord is sufficiently annoyed to be trying to get you out, it is likely to want to do so whether or not you are technically or legally in the wrong.

Where a local authority or a development corporation is the landlord, it *may* be possible to challenge this sort of attitude, in law. You will certainly need legal assistance to do so (see Chapter 12).

This is not true of housing association landlords. In their case, or if the local authority or development corporation cannot be challenged on the point in *law*, you should remember that all of these public landlords are vulnerable to publicity which will be adverse if they are acting maliciously or in a way more to be expected from the private sector.

Where they start out trying to evict you because they believe you have done something wrong – brought in a sharer or sub-tenant without consent – but it can be shown that you have not committed a breach of your agreement, it may well be considered malicious or unacceptable conduct to carry on regardless. The eviction would be because of *their* mistake (in the way they prepared the agreement, or how they have handled matters since), not *yours*. This is the sort of circumstance where a tenants' association or other community group may help, or where publicity can dissuade the landlord from proceeding (see Chapter 11).

5: The Right to Buy

Is the right to buy available to secure tenants and non-secure occupiers?

No. The right to buy is only available to secure tenants. Public landlords are sometimes able to sell to non-secure occupiers, in which case the sale will be on the same terms as under the right to buy. However, this will be a voluntary sale and it is entirely in the discretion of the landlord whether or not to agree. The only way to find out is to ask the landlord!

If you are a non-secure occupier, then, you should not trouble with this chapter at all, *unless* your landlord has agreed to sell to you, in which case the chapter will be a useful guide to the terms on which you will be allowed to buy.

Do I need a solicitor to exercise the right to buy?

As a matter of law, no one has to have a solicitor when buying somewhere to live. However, there are many, many complexities about purchasing houses and flats, and to buy without the assistance of a solicitor is a risky exercise.

This is just as true when buying from a public landlord as otherwise. Once you start the process of buying, you will have both to complete, and be sent, lengthy and detailed forms, relating to your rights, the price you will have to pay, how much "discount" (see below) you will get, the terms of the transaction and perhaps mortgage as well. You will not find it easy to complete all these forms, or to check whether what you are being offered – by way of sale or mortgage – is what you are entitled to. A mistake can be very costly.

It is not possible in this book to take you through every detail, at every stage, because the different possibilities which may apply in your case could make this chapter as long as the whole of the rest of the book! You are therefore strongly advised to use a lawyer when exercising the right to buy (see Chapter 12).

If you buy with the help of a mortgage, from or through your landlord, the amount you will get may include an amount for the cost of a lawyer (see page 74). You can also be given an outright grant for the costs of the help you need when buying (see page 72).

Are both houses and flats for sale?

Yes. Subject to the exceptions described below, you will be entitled to either a freehold (i.e. outright ownership) or long lease of a house, or a long lease of a flat.

Do I have the right to buy?

You have the right to buy if you are a secure tenant, and certain preconditions are fulfilled. In addition, the transaction must not be "exempt".

A. Preconditions

You must have two years' public tenancy before claiming the right to buy. Being one of joint tenants (see Chapter 1) counts the same as if you were the only tenant. If you are a joint tenant in your present premises, and both or all of you wish to buy, only one of you need prove qualification.

It is not that difficult to "clock up" two years, but we have to consider how time is calculated, in some detail, because we will refer to it again, when discussing how much "discount" you will get on the purchase (see page 70).

Time as a public tenant is not the same as two years as a secure tenant, with your present landlord. Any period as a secure tenant will qualify, regardless of whether or not with your present landlord, and regardless of whether this is a continuous period as a secure tenant or several periods broken up by periods when you were not a secure tenant.

Thus, if you were once a public tenant, for more than two years, and then spent a period, even perhaps of years, for example abroad or in an owner-occupied property, before being rehoused as a secure tenant, you will qualify the day your new tenancy starts.

You cannot rely, however, on your own periods of time – or those of another where you are allowed to take them into account (see below) – when the landlord was a housing association which was (at the time you were its tenant) either a charity or a housing assocation which has never received public funds for its work (see Chapter 2).

Periods spent with Scottish or Northern Ireland public landlords equivalent to those classed as public landlords in this book (see Chapter 2) qualify as public tenancy. If you – or a spouse (see below) – were a member of the armed forces and were provided with accommodation by them, it counts as public tenancy.

In some cases, you can rely not only on your own periods as a public tenant, but someone else's period as a public tenant. You can add the periods your spouse – or a deceased spouse – has spent as a public-sector tenant, or as the spouse of a public-sector tenant, or your own periods as the spouse of a public-sector tenant. This includes deceased spouses. In these cases, however, you can only add "spouse-periods" if they were periods when you and spouse were living together, and if the spouse whose periods of time you want to add has died, if you were living together at the time of death.

In addition, if you succeeded to the tenancy or took it over by way of family transfer (see Chapter 3), while you cannot add the period of the person you took it over from (usually, a parent), you can add the period you lived in the property before you took over the tenancy. This is only so, however, provided that (a) it is a period since you turned 16, and (b) there was no more than a two-year break in the period you want to claim.

B. Exemptions

There are a number of exemptions, when you will not have the the right to buy, even though you are a secure tenant.

(1) The landlord is a housing association which is a charity, or which has at no time received public funds for its work.

(2) A court order has been made against you, which requires you to give up occupation at a specific date (see Chapter 7).

(3) There is a bankruptcy petition pending against you, or your joint tenant, or an order or arrangements have been made relating to bankruptcy.

(4) Your premises are part of, or are within the grounds of, a non-housing building (for example a school), or a cemetery, and the tenancy was granted in connection with a job.

(5) The premises have features which are substantially different from normal premises, designed to make them suitable for occupation by the physically disabled, *and* one of three further conditions is fulfilled.

(a) the premises were built like that, or if the premises were converted from an existing building, have had those features since conversion;

(b) if the features were added later, they include one or more of the following: not less than 7.5 additional square metres of floor space; an additional bathroom or shower-room; or a lift;

(c) if neither (a) nor (b) applies, the premises are part of a group of premises let out for occupation by the physically disabled, and special support facilities (such as a warden) are provided nearby for their benefit.

(6) The premises are part of a group of properties let for occupation by those who are suffering or have suffered from mental disorders, and facilities (such as a warden) are provided nearby for their benefit.

(7) The premises are part of a group of properties which are particularly suitable for occupation by the elderly, and are normally let for occupation by the elderly, and facilities (such as a warden) are provided nearby for their benefit. The facilities must include *either* a resident warden *or* a system for calling a non-resident warden plus a common-room for the residents to use. ''Particularly suitable'' means in relation to where the properties are, their size, design, heating and other features.

(8) Although not part of a group of old people's dwellings, the property is particularly suitable (see above) for an elderly person, and was let for occupation by *either* an elderly person *or* a physically handicapped person. This exemption applies only when an application is made by the landlord to the Secretary of State for the Environment.

(9) If the landlord does not itself own the freehold, there is no right to buy unless at the date you make your claim, the landlord has a sufficient time left on its lease. Sufficient time, for this purpose, depends on whether what you are buying is a house or a flat. If a house, the landlord must have at least twenty-one years left to run on its lease; if a flat, at least fifty years.

(10) When the full procedure towards right to buy has been completed (see below), the landlord is entitled to refuse to sell if you are four or more weeks in arrears with your rent, or any other payment due as tenant (for example, a service or heating charge – see Chapter 8), unless you first clear the debt.

What will I get under the right to buy?

If you occupy a house and the landlord owns the freehold, you will be able to buy the freehold yourself. If you occupy a house but the landlord only has a lease, you will be able to buy a 125-year lease, or a lease which is five days shorter than that of your landlord, whichever is the less.

In the case of a lease of a house – but *not* of a flat – there are additional provisions which will allow you to buy out the landlord's lease, and any other leases between you and the freeholder, and eventually purchase the freehold itself.

These provisions are contained in the Leasehold Reform Act 1967. They apply to people who own private leases of twenty-one years or more, and the subject is treated as one of owner-occupation. If you want to know more about this, take advice (see Chapter 12).

If you occupy a flat, you will only get a lease, even if the landlord owns the freehold. Your lease will be for 125 years, unless one of two circumstances applies.

If the landlord has already sold a lease under the right to buy to another tenant in the block, your lease can be shorter, so as to come to an end at the same time as the lease of that other tenant.

If the landlord does not own the freehold of the block, your lease can also be shorter than 125 years, i.e. it can be five days less than the period left to run on your landlord's lease.

In one circumstance, in addition to these possibilities, you may be entitled to something called a "shared ownership lease", which means that you are the part owner of a long lease, and part still the tenant. This will be referred to below.

Will I be able to buy everything that I am renting?

You will be able to buy the house or flat you live in, of course. You will also be able to buy land let together with it unless it is agricultural land, of more than two acres.

If you have had the use of any other land, such as a neighbouring field, or a garage, you are entitled to ask for it to be included in the sale and the landlord is bound to agree if it is reasonable that you should do so. You can make this request at any time before the sale is complete.

Can the landlord make the sale on any terms it wishes?

No. The terms of the sale – whether freehold or long lease – are tightly defined by law. There *will* be a term allowing the landlord to reclaim part of your "discount" (see next answer), if you resell within five years.

If you buy a lease of a *flat*, there will be a term entitling the landlord to claim a "service charge" from you, in respect of a share of its later costs in the block as a whole, i.e. common parts, facilities and structure. If you buy the freehold or a lease of a *house*, there may also be a term to similar effect, relevant to the services or facilities on an estate.

In the case of a *flat*, neither the service-charge part of the lease nor any other part can require you to pay any money in respect of subsequent repairs to the block as a whole, if those repairs are required as a result of a structural defect, *unless* one of two conditions is fulfilled.

Those conditions are: *either* that at the time the landlord first notifies you of sale price (see next question), it *also* warns you of the existence of such a defect, and provides you with an estimate of the (then current) cost of remedying it, *or* that the landlord does not find out about it until ten years after you buy the lease.

The purpose of this is to prevent landlords concealing the fact that, soon after you buy, you will have to share (through the service charge) in massive, additional costs. Obviously, there is no "concealment" if the landlord did not know, and the landlord is treated as not knowing if it does not find out for ten years *after* the transaction.

The lease also cannot require you to pay a service charge for costs of insuring the block as a whole, unless it *also* entitles you to see the actual policy. This is because a mortage company will normally require *you* to insure, but may not do so if it can see the landlord's policy. It will save you paying insurance twice over: your own, and part of the landlord's.

There *may* be a term either preventing you from selling without the consent of the landlord, or else requiring you to offer to sell the premises back to the landlord, if you want to dispose of the property within ten years. This will only happen – if at all – in special areas:

a property in a National Park, an area designated as of outstanding natural beauty, or an area specially designated for the purposes of these provisions.

If the provision is one requiring consent to disposal, it lasts indefinitely, but consent cannot be withheld if the sale is to a class of person defined for these purposes, in outline being those who already live or work in or near to the area in question.

These provisions are designed to prevent sale of public properties to tenants who then sell on to middle-class people wanting a second home in the countryside.

In the case of a lease, whether of house or flat, there will be a requirement to pay a ground rent, but this will be no more than £10 per year (except in the case of a shared ownership lease, see page 76).

Other terms may be agreed between you and the landlord, although only so far as what the landlord wants is reasonable, and a dispute over whether or not the landlord is entitled to insist on one term or another may be referred to court (see Chapter 12).

What will I have to pay?

You have the pay the market value of the property, *less* a discount. The market value is calculated as at the date of your claim to buy, so that subsequent delays will not cause a price rise.

The landlord will state how much it thinks the market value is, and if you disagree, there is a right to refer the matter to the District Valuer, who is an independent official, not employed by the authority. You have to appeal within three months of this notification of the landlord's asking price.

When calculating the market value, any improvements you may have carried out (see Chapter 10) are to be disregarded, as are those of someone from whom you took over the tenancy, *other* than under the right to exchange. You may, accordingly, have to pay for the value of improvements which were carried out by someone you exchanged with.

You would be well advised to seek the assistance of a surveyor and valuer before deciding whether the property you live in is worth buying, or worth what is being asked for it. His or her report will be valuable material to show the District Valuer, especially if there are latent defects.

The discount is the main attraction. You will be entitled to discount based on the qualifying years described above. That is why it was important to set out those details. You will get 32 per cent off the market price for two years' qualifying time, plus 1 per cent for each additional full year, to a maximum of 60 per cent (i.e. thirty years in all).

If you have bought under the right to buy before, and are now trying for a second time, any discount you got then (less any amount of it you had to pay back – see below) will be deducted from your present discount.

In the case of relatively new property, the Secretary of State may set a maximum discount, reflecting what the property cost or what has been spent on it, which may be less than described above.

Can I get the discount in cash, and buy somewhere else?

Normally, no. All you can do is buy, then sell at a later date: if you sell within five years, you will have to pay some of the discount back (see next answer).

However, the tenants of charitable housing associations, who are exempt from the right to buy (see page 66), can benefit from a scheme which allows them to do exactly this: buy somewhere else, and receive a contribution to the purchase price, equal to the discount they would have qualified for if they had been entitled to buy. The details of this scheme are too lengthy to be included in this book. If you are the tenant of a charitable association, ask your landlord for the details, or otherwise find out from your nearest local authority, or from the Housing Corporation (see Chapter 12).

When will I have to pay back the discount?

If you dispose of the property, otherwise than by a family transaction, within five years of buying, you have to repay the whole of the discount, *less* 20 per cent for each full year of occupation since purchase. Family transaction includes transfer on death or divorce, but in other cases you should seek advice as to whether or not it will be protected from discount repayment.

Can I buy jointly with others?

Yes. All joint tenants share the right to buy, and indeed if all the joint tenants do not want to buy, one or less than all cannot go ahead without the consent of the "non-purchaser". It is only necessary for *one* out of the joint tenants to qualify, for *all* of them to be able to buy.

Secondly, you can insist that the sale be not only to you, but instead to you plus up to three other members of your family (see Chapter 2), although in the case of someone other than your spouse (legally married), they will have to be people who have lived with you in the property for a year before you make the claim.

This may be very helpful in two ways. First of all, if the member of your family has himself or herself been a public tenant somewhere else, he or she will have qualifying time, *which may be greater than your own*. This will not be *added* to yours, but you will be entitled to the higher amount, i.e. the discount will equal the highest discount any of the joint purchasers can claim.

Secondly, it may entitle you to a greater amount of mortgage, either from a private company or from the landlord (see below).

Can I get a mortgage?

Yes. You can buy with a mortgage from a building society, or a bank, if there is one who will lend you the money to do so. These bodies will not usually lend on leases of less than thirty years, but it will not be often that you will be entitled to less (see above).

If you borrow from a private society or bank, you will be charged for the mortgage service (i.e. survey, preparation of documents) as well, of course, as having to pay back what you borrow. Your landlord *may* give you a grant to meet this charge, but only to a limit set by the government.

What a private society or bank will lend depends on two things. First, it depends on what they think you can afford to pay. This is an income calculation, and as a rule of thumb they tend to lend two-and-a-half times your annual income, plus one times the annual income of any additional purchaser, such as your spouse, or another member of your family (see above).

Secondly, what they lend will depend on what *they* think is the value of the property, and sometimes they will only lend up to 90 per cent of that amount. What they think the property is worth may be less than what the landlord has asked for, or even than the District Valuer has decided. It is extremely unlikely, however, to be less than the amount you need, because of your discount.

When a private building society or bank is lending, they will conduct their own survey. They may release a copy of this survey to you. If they release it to you, and unless they disclaim even this much responsibility, you may rely on what it says, but it is important to note that the questions they are interested in are different from those which will concern you.

Thus, they will be concerned principally with value, which includes the structural condition, and only those aspects of disrepair which may cause the structure to deteriorate. (They may make their offer of mortgage conditional on your carrying out repairs, within a fixed time. They may hold back some of the purchase price until you have done so.)

The questions which will concern you will be wider, and you will want to know everything that you are going to have to do. It is still worthwhile, then, to have your own survey carried out (see above).

If they do not release a copy of the report to you but still make an offer, you know that they think the property is worth at least what they will lend. However, in this case *you* are not entitled to rely on the (unseen) surveyor's report as a guarantee or opinion that the purchase is worthwhile, and you must have your own carried out.

If you cannot – or do not want to – get a mortgage from the private sector, you are entitled to one from your own landlord, except in the case of a housing association, when the mortgage is provided by the Housing Corporation (see Chapters 2 and 12). The landlord (or Corporation) is entitled to charge a fee for this mortgage service, but only for the costs of preparing the documentation, and only to a limit set by the government, currently £50.

The landlord or Corporation will not have their own, additional survey carried out for the purpose of the mortgage, so you will be more than ever reliant on your own surveyor.

If you want a public mortgage in this way, you have to apply for it within three months either of the landlord's notice which tells you, among other things, what it wants you to pay for the property (see below), or of the conclusion of an appeal to the District Valuer (see below). The landlord can, however, extend this period, and so can a court if the landlord refuses. These time-limits, and the appropriate application form, will be included in the landlord's notice.

If there has been an appeal to the District Valuer, you will again be advised of the right to a mortgage and provided with an application form, when notified of the result of the appeal.

The amount you will be entitled to by way of mortgage will be decided by reference to what you can afford to pay, determined according to regulations prepared for this purpose by the government, dealing with different situations, including purchase by more than one person.

Value will not be in issue, because the provider of mortgage is also usually the landlord (or in the case of a housing association, the Housing Corporation acting on behalf of the landlord), who has decided the sale price (or is bound by the decision of the District Valuer). Then, the discount is to be deducted.

If you are not limited by the income factor, the amount you will be entitled to receive by way of mortgage is the *full* purchase price (i.e. market value less discount), *plus* any amount which you spend arranging the mortgage which the landlord (or Corporation) agrees to advance you, *plus* the costs which you may be charged for the mortgage service (see above).

We may call this absolute maximum "100 per cent + ". If your income limit does not entitle you to "100 per cent + ", what will your position be? You may, of course, have savings with which to make up the difference and – although this is to be strongly discouraged – you *could* borrow the balance elsewhere.

(It is not recommended for this reason. Because the landlord or Corporation will be giving you a mortgage, if you run into financial difficulties they will be able to take the property back, and so their loan is safe. If you borrow the balance from someone else, they cannot enjoy this extensive security against repayment. The most they can do is place a "second mortgage" on the property, i.e. getting their money back *after* any debt to the "first mortgage" – landlord, or Corporation – has been cleared. For this reason, conventional building societies and banks will not lend the balance.

You would have to borrow from a "fringe" bank or financial institution, and these often charge notoriously – cripplingly – high interest rates.)

If you cannot raise the balance in any sensible alternative way, then, you might think you have to let the purchase go. Not so. There are no less than two ways you can still acquire an interest in your home. You will be advised of these, and provided with application forms, when given the result of your mortgage application, if that result amounts to less than the 100 per cent + I have described above.

First of all, for a payment of £100, you can place a deposit on the property, for up to two years, which "freezes" the value, at the price determined. This means that you have two years in which to raise the balance (or your income may increase, allowing you a larger mortgage), without the risk of a price rise.

Secondly, having placed your £100 deposit, you can, instead of waiting to see whether you can "catch up", ask to be granted a "shared ownership lease", and the landlord has to grant you one. This involves buying "part" of the property now and deferring the balance.

There is no such thing as a shared ownership freehold, so if what you are buying is a house, of which you would normally get the freehold, if you take this course of action you will get a lease instead (though later, you will be able to acquire the freehold in any event – see below).

What is a shared ownership lease?

This is a relatively novel idea, sometimes called "half-and-half", sometimes called "equity sharing". Basically, you get a lease, which will be of the same length as any other lease under right to buy (see page 68), and on the same terms as otherwise, save in one respect.

That is, you only pay a part of the purchase price, say 50 per cent, and you carry on paying the balance of your rent, in this example also 50 per cent. If you bought 75 per cent, you would pay 25 per cent rent. Rent is calculated in the same way as any other secure tenancy (see Chapter 8), but you are only charged a percentage.

Under shared ownership, you *have* to buy at least 50 per cent to begin with, and *at present* you can only have higher amounts of 62.5 per cent, 75 per cent, 87.5 per cent. These proportions may be changed by the government. You do, however, have the right to go on buying additional shares, in the same 12.5 per cent units, until you have acquired 100 per cent.

Whether on your initial 50 per cent (or higher) purchase, or on the purchase of a later share, you are given a discount in the same percentage as if it was normal right to buy (see page 71).

You can buy additional shares at any time. However, what you pay for shares bought at a later date is the appropriate proportion of the *then* market value (decided in the same way as a normal right to buy – see page 70). In other words, your later shares may be at a higher price, because property prices have risen.

This is one of the drawbacks to shared ownership. It is compensated for (but not necessarily fully – this depends on how much prices rise) by the fact that you will get a discount entitlement calculated up to the time of the additional share, i.e. qualifying time does not stop at initial purchase.

The other drawback is that you take on liabilities *as if* you had become the owner under normal right to buy, which include repairing obligations. (See page 79, under Should I buy?) If you defer purchase, or leave the issue aside altogether, you remain the tenant, and the landlord keeps these burdens (see Chapter 10).

If you proceed with shared ownership, and eventually acquire 100 per cent of the interest, the landlord has to give you the freehold, free of charge, in exactly the same circumstances as those in which you would have been entitled to the freehold on normal right to buy.

If what you would have been entitled to on normal right to buy is a lease, you will get a lease of the same length once you purchase 100 per cent under shared ownership.

How do I pay for shared ownership?

In exactly the same way as normal right to buy. Some private-sector building societies and banks will lend on shared ownership but, it must be said, not many.

You will only be able to get a public mortgage (see above) if your income limit amounts to at least the initial 50 per cent (see page 76) unless, of course, you can make up the balance yourself. *(You are not advised to borrow the balance privately: see page 75.)*

At any time, you can ask for additional shares, and reconsideration of your mortgage entitlement, with which to pay for another 12.5 per cent (or 25 per cent, or 37.5 per cent). If this "mortgage review" shows that you have enough income to buy out the whole of what remains outstanding, you can be required to "finish off" and buy it all out.

Can I sell a shared ownership lease?

You can transfer the shared ownership lease in the same circumstances as you could transfer without having to pay back discount (see page 72). Otherwise, you cannot transfer it at all without "completing" the purchase, i.e. buying out the remaining shares.

Once you have bought 100 per cent, you are in the same position as under normal right to buy. The restrictions on sale which may apply in particular areas (see page 70) will also apply to shared ownership leases.

How do I exercise the right to buy?

All the public-sector landlords whose secure tenants have the right to buy have forms on which you can apply. They are bound to supply you with one within seven days of a request.

The procedure starts with a form from you. Within a period of four to eight weeks – depending on whether or not you are relying on qualifying time with a different landlord from your present landlord – the landlord must reply admitting or denying your right.

In the case of a property which *may* be exempt from right to buy because it is an elderly person's dwelling for which application for exemption must be made to the Secretary of State (see page 67), the landlord should tell you that it has made the application, and an admission of your right is "without prejudice" to the decision of the Secretary of State's decision, i.e. if he or she grants the exemption you then "lose" your right.

If you disagree with the landlord's decision (which means with the landlord's denial of your right to buy), you should take advice on how to challenge it (see Chapter 12), or you can complain directly to the

Secretary of State for the Environment, whose department may intervene on your behalf or provide you with the assistance you need.

Within a further eight weeks in the case of a freehold, or twelve weeks in the case of a lease, the landlord should write you setting out its view of the transaction. This will contain such details as its view of price, terms, discount, property to be included, etc.

The landlord will also advise you of the right to refer the price to the District Valuer, and of the right to claim a mortgage, and provide a form with which to do so.

If you use this mortgage form, when the landlord replies to it you will be advised of its view of how much you are entitled to, how that has been calculated, and, if the amount is less than 100 per cent + (see page 74), your rights to defer completion and to buy a shared ownership lease (see page 76), and again the landlord will provide forms on which to apply.

You would be well advised to seek legal help on the completion of all these forms, as an error may cost you money or result in a purchase which is not on the best terms you are entitled to (see Chapter 12).

Can I back out of right to buy?

Yes. At any time before the transaction is completed, you can withdraw your claim. You can, if you like, restart as soon as you want to do so, though of course at risk of a higher price.

If I cannot make up my mind whether or not to proceed, how long can I remain undecided?

There can be no pressure on you to "get on with it" until all the relevant questions, including as to mortgage, have been completed, although there are time-limits for exercising rights as they arise in the course of these proceedings (and of which you will be advised as relevant in each of the landlord's forms).

Once all the outstanding issues have been resolved, the landlord is entitled to start a "completion process". This, however, is extremely relaxed. It must first provide you with a "warning notice", asking you either to identify what you think has still not been resolved that is relevant to the transaction, or to complete it.

You get nine months before the next step can be taken, which is a notice to complete, requiring you to conclude the transaction. Even so, there is another nine months before the landlord is entitled to treat the application as if it had been withdrawn by you, for non-completion.

If you have exercised the right to defer completion (see page 75), by paying £100 deposit, the landlord cannot start this completion pressure until the two years you have "bought" have expired. If you are treated as having withdrawn your application, you can recommence at once, subject only to the risk of an increased price.

Should I buy?

This is entirely a personal decision. The deal sounds, and in many cases is, very attractive indeed, perhaps the best "government handout" you will ever see in your life.

The difficulties are twofold, and very different. First of all, you have to consider whether you really do want to own the property you live in. There are many reasons why it may not be a "good buy".

For example, you might find that it is *harder* to move at a later date, because no one wants to buy the property, than if you remained a tenant and secured a transfer or exchange (see Chapter 3). You have become *more*, not *less*, securely tied to your own particular plot of ground.

Then, you will find that mortgage costs are only the *beginning* of what you will be paying instead of rent. If you have a lease, especially of a flat, you will have service charges (see Chapter 8). If you buy a house, *you*, not the landlord, will be responsible for repairing costs, insurance, external decoration and so on.

Then there is the condition itself. You will be well advised to have your own surveyor's report, because what may appear a good-quality property, even to you who live in it, may in fact have serious deficiencies.

None of this is intended to discourage, merely to advise caution. You will not be glad you bought if the end consequence is not being able to move, or to afford to pay the mortgage, resulting perhaps (and as *often*, not occasionally, happens) in homelessness, in turn deemed intentional (see Chapter 1).

The other general consideration is political. From the description of why you should be cautious, it will already be clear that the "best" deals will be houses, with gardens. The present government is not providing money with which to replace housing sold under the right to buy. It follows that purchases of houses with gardens is gradually leading to a public sector which is increasingly of the *inferior* quality stock, i.e. houses without gardens, odd inner-city properties, flats, especially in tower blocks, or both houses and flats on environmentally unpopular estates.

I am not suggesting that you should not buy for this reason, only that you should think about whether it might not be socially preferable, if you have the money, to buy somewhere else, outside the public sector.

Unless, however, you are the tenant of a charitable association who in any event *cannot* buy, but who can "take your discount with you", it is, of course, a "social preference" that will clearly cost you dear (your discount).

6: Terms of Tenancy

What will the terms of my tenancy be?

That will depend on what has been "agreed". Of course, there is rarely discussion between a prospective public tenant and the landlord as to what terms are appropriate to a particular tenancy: this really only happens in the case of unusual lettings, such as fixed-term, or for some special purpose.

Rather, there will be either a standard form of tenancy agreement, or a rent book or card containing terms, or even a mere sheet which indicates the obligations of both landlord and tenant, or perhaps tenant alone. Public tenancy agreements have been severely criticised recently, particular by the National and Welsh Consumer Councils, on this among other grounds.

Secure tenants have to be given their terms of tenancy in writing, except those terms described below as "implied by law".

Can the landlord put any term it likes in the agreement?

In principle, yes. However, nothing in the agreement can override terms which Parliament has said shall apply, nor in some circumstances those which will be implied by law. Furthermore, if the landlord includes pointless or ridiculous terms, it may well find that the courts do not enforce them (see Chapter 7).

What terms does the law imply?

In the case of *all* tenancies, secure and not secure, the law implies a term that the tenant will have what is known as "quiet enjoyment" of the premises so long as the tenancy lasts.

This means that the use and enjoyment of the premises has been given to you, and that the landlord will not interfere with them, other than so far as the law expressly permits (i.e. when the landlord is entitled to terminate the tenancy, and/or evict, and when the landlord enjoys a right of entry, such as to repair or improve – see Chapter 10).

Similarly, there is implied into all tenancies a promise that the landlord will not use adjoining property, which it does not rent out, in such a way as to destroy your own proper use of the premises (for example, by placing a noisy factory right next door).

Where your home is part of a larger unit, perhaps in a block of flats, the law will usually imply a term that the landlord will maintain the common parts – stairs, halls, corridors, lifts, etc. – in a usable state. A landlord *can* exclude this term by an express statement in the agreement, but this would be unusual.

Under a *licence* (see Chaper 2), these terms are not implied in quite the same way as under a tenancy, but as a general proposition the courts will treat the landlord as in the same position, because the landlord has to keep the premises let to you fit for the purpose for which they were let.

In the main, that which would amount to a breach of the terms described above would mean that the landlord was failing to do so.

These are the principal "general" terms implied by law, but in addition, there are the terms which Parliament has said shall apply. These are the repairing terms which are described in Chapter 10; and, in relation to *secure* tenancies, there are also terms concerning assignment and exchange (see Chapter 3) and permission to take in subtenants and lodgers (Chapter 4).

How do I find out the terms of my tenancy?

If you have a written tenancy agreement, or a rent book containing terms, these will be the "terms of the tenancy". If there is a written document, which outlines obligations, on either part, the law will treat this as evidence of what the terms were intended to be, although often these are so vaguely worded that it would not be correct to describe them as "actual terms".

In the case of secure tenants, landlords *have* to do two things. They have to provide a written statement of terms, *other* than those described above as implied by law, and *other* than what is described in Chapter 10 as the "principal repairing obligation" on a landlord.

In addition, the landlord has to publish information to explain the *effect* of its tenancy terms, *and* of the principal repairing obligation (see Chapter 10), *and* of most of the other rights of secure tenants described in this book.

It does *not* have to include the implied terms described above, or the rights to housing described in Chapter 1, or the other rights which are described in this book as applying *both* to secure tenants *and* to non-secure occupiers.

However, it is a matter for the landlord what it considers the best way to provide this information, i.e. how much information to provide, and in what language (which must be designed "to explain in simple terms").

The information must be kept up to date. A copy of this information must be provided to all secure tenants on the grant of the tenancy, or as soon as practicable thereafter.

Can the landlord change the terms of the tenancy?

The position is different for non-secure occupiers, and for secure tenants.

A. Non-Secure Occupiers

In the case of a *non-secure* tenant or licensee, it will depend on whether the agreement is *periodic* or *fixed-term* (see Chapter 2). If the agreement is periodic, it is no problem for the landlord to bring it to an end, even in order to issue you with a new agreement, i.e. containing the new terms (see Chapter 7).

If the agreement is fixed-term, then unless it contains a provision allowing the landlord to vary its terms (which it may do for, say, rent or other charges) the whole point of granting you a right of occupation, for a fixed period of time, on stated terms, would be defeated if the landlord could change the terms whenever it wanted to do so.

If, therefore, you do not agree to the change, the landlord cannot impose the change on you. If, however, you are coming towards the end of your agreement, you will wish to consider whether failure to agree might affect your chances of getting a new agreement, and whether or not this is important to you.

Also, if you *break* a term of your agreement, the landlord may be able to bring even a fixed-term tenancy or licence to an end (see Chapter 7), in which case it might be prepared to let you stay on, but on new terms. In effect, it may be able to use your breach to compel you to agree.

If you still do not wish to agree, you may, of course, be willing to take your chances in court, because if you break a term of a fixed-term tenancy, and the landlord takes you to court, it does not *necessarily* mean you will have to quit (see Chapter 7).

B. Secure Tenants

If you are a *secure* tenant, your position is a bit stronger. First of all, there are certain terms which cannot be changed; secondly, before any change in the terms, there are procedures which the landlord must follow, which give you an opportunity to make representations, perhaps preventing the change.

The landlord cannot vary any of the terms which Parliament has said shall apply. Nor can the premises which have been let be varied – by reducing the size of your premises, taking away a room, etc. Thus, if a garden or a garage has been let as part of the tenancy, there cannot be a variation to take it away; if, however, the garage or garden was let by a separate, even if simultaneous, agreement, then it is not part of the tenancy, and so not subject to the restrictions on variation.

Otherwise, a variation can always be agreed: you might not mind or might even welcome the change.

As regards rent, the tenancy agreement itself may permit a variation in the rent charged, or for rates rises, or for services (see Chapter 8). This may be so under either a periodic or a fixed-term tenancy (see Chapter 2). If there is such a provision, the change can take place in accordance with its terms.

If the tenancy agreement does not permit change, the landlord cannot increase the charges for a fixed-term tenancy, until it comes to an end. At this time, either the landlord and the tenant will agree a new fixed term, or there will be an automatic periodic tenancy (see Chapter 7). If a new fixed term is agreed, new charges will be agreed; otherwise, the landlord must use the procedure for varying periodic rents.

If – or once – the tenancy is periodic, the landlord can vary rent or service charges by a notice, which must give either four weeks' warning, or warning of one period of the tenancy, whichever is longer. (Thus, four weeks for a weekly or fortnightly tenancy; one month for a monthly tenancy, etc.)

Turning to variation of terms *other* than rent or for services, these, too, can be altered by notice of variation, of the same length.

However, in *these* cases, before serving the notice of variation, the landlord must also serve a preliminary or consultative notice, which specifies what is proposed, and what effect it will have, and inviting comment within a reasonable time (which must be stated in the notice).

Before proceeding with the notice of variation itself, the landlord must consider any comments thus made. If there is a tenants' association in your area, you would do well to see if others are commenting, or objecting, and co-ordinate or co-operate with them (see Chapter 11).

In any case, when a notice of variation is served, whether for rent/services, or otherwise, you are entitled to respond with notice to quit (see Chapter 7), in which case the variation will not take effect, but you will have to leave – unless (a) you change your mind, (b) the landlord permits you to withdraw your notice, and (c) the landlord confirms the withdrawal *in writing.*

Do not do this unless you have somewhere else to move to (for certain), or without qualified advice (see Chapter 12), and without considering the consequences seriously, even if, for example, you think you cannot afford a new rent. You may well find not only that you have made yourself homeless, but that you are homeless intentionally (see Chapter 1), and that the local authority does not have to find you somewhere else.

Instead, take advice as to whether anything can done to protect you against the change, such as by way of housing benefit (see Chapter 9).

In addition to these provisions for "individual" variation, there may have to be wider "consultation" on matters of "housing management", likely to affect groups of secure tenants as a whole. This provision is mainly concerned with tenants' associations, and is considered in Chapter 11.

7: Security of Tenure

What is "security of tenure"?

Security of tenure is the right to remain in the premises, even if the landlord wants you out. Every lawful occupier has *some* security of tenure: at the least, what the agreement is for – which could, for example, in the case of a hostel, be as little as a day or a week, or could, in the case of a long tenancy, be ninety-nine years!

We are principally concerned in this chapter with the security of tenure of secure tenants (i.e. including licensees: see Chapter 2), who will usually be periodic tenants, i.e. from week to week or month to month, or who may have fairly short fixed-term leases, such as three or five years.

Notwithstanding the shortness of these *agreed* periods, the law confers on secure tenants the right to remain in occupation for life (and, indeed, for a member of the family to succeed and take over for his or her life too – see Chapter 3). The landlord can only make a secure tenant quit in one of the circumstances described in this chapter. That is what security of tenure means.

In addition, non-secure occupiers have a *little* bit of security, namely that agreed, plus the very limited rights to remain in occupation, while the landlord follows the correct procedure towards an eviction (which can add a few weeks or even months).

Secure Tenants

When can the landlord make me leave?

The "grounds" on which a landlord can make you leave may be considered in *four* groups.

Group 1

If your tenancy ceases to be secure, you will fall into the category of non-secure occupier. Your rights will be much fewer than as a secure tenant, and it will not be difficult for the landlord to make you leave.

(1) You may cease to be a secure tenant if you stop occupying the

premises as your only or main home (see Chapter 2). If there is a joint tenancy, the secure tenancy will last so long as at least one of the joint tenants continues to use the premises as an only or main home.

The secure tenancy will continue, however, even if you cease to live there, if the reason you have left home is because of a matrimonial breakdown, and your spouse remains in occupation (as an only or main home) *until* the divorce becomes final. Once the divorce becomes final, he or she is no longer your spouse, so this exception will not apply.

If you are the non-tenant spouse, therefore, you will want to make sure that the tenancy is transferred into your name *before* the divorce becomes final (see Chapter 3).

(2) The secure tenancy will also cease if you *sublet* the *whole* of the premises, whether at one time or by a series of sublettings until the whole has been sublet (see Chapter 4).

If you have sublet the whole of the premises, without intending to return, you would not, of course, be using the premises as an only or main home, in any event. You might have done it planning to come back. It does not matter. Once you have sublet the whole of the premises, the tenancy has ceased to be secure and it does not become secure again just because you reoccupy.

This is different from taking in lodgers or licensees (see Chapter 4). If you have to go away for a time, you might want people in occupation of the whole of the premises, not under formal sub-tenancies, but under an informal arrangement, to look after the premises for you, perhaps pay the rent and other outgoings, etc.

If you do this, you do not automatically cease to be a secure tenant but you still run the risk that it will look as if you have abandoned use as an only or main home. What you have to do is to make sure *both* that you leave in the premises "evidence" of continued occupation, such as furniture and other belongings, *and* can demonstrate that it was, and has remained, your intention to return.

There is little risk in leaving the premises for a period of time while members of your family, who normally live with you, remain in occupation, so long as you still intend to return. They may be treated as "evidence" of your continued occupation. The longer the time goes on, the better the reason for the absence will need to be, and the stronger the chances will become that you will be treated as having left.

Group 2

If the landlord can prove one of eight circumstances, it can seek an order for your eviction. In addition to proving these circumstances, however, it must *also* prove that it is *reasonable* to make the order. It is the court which will decide *both* whether they have proved the circumstances *and* whether it is reasonable to make you leave.

What "reasonable" means will be different in every case. For example, one of the circumstances is arrears of rent. If the arrears are small, or there is an acceptable explanation (such as that you did not know about, or have not been receiving, your Housing Benefit – see Chapter 9), you should not be made to go, although your right to remain will be conditional on clearing the arrears at an agreed rate.

Similarly, if you have broken another condition of your tenancy, but either it is an unimportant condition or the breach was small, or "technical" (see Chapters 3 and 4), you should not be made to go, although again this may be conditional on rectifying the breach – for instance, evicting an illegal sub-tenant.

If you have been a nuisance to neighbours, again unless the nuisance has been severe you ought to be allowed one chance to remain, on terms that you do not repeat the nuisance.

In every case, however, whether or not the failure on your part is serious enough to merit an order is a matter for the county court judge, and it is very hard to predict what he or she will think. And even when the fault is minor, if it is not the first occasion you might find that you are evicted immediately.

If possession proceedings are commenced against you (see page 94), you ought to take advice as soon as possible, and consider being represented at the court (see Chapter 12).

The eight circumstances are:

(1) You are in arrears with your rent, or have broken some other term of the tenancy (see Chapter 6).

(2) You have been, or someone living with you has been, a nuisance or annoyance to neighbours, or been convicted of using the premises or allowing them to be used for immoral or illegal purposes.

(3) You have allowed the premises, including the garden, or the common parts of a building in which a flat is situated, to deteriorate, because of neglect or damage. Deterioration can also result from the actions of someone living with you. If this is a lodger or sub-tenant (see Chapter 4), an order should only be made against you if you have not done all that you reasonably can be expected to have done to evict him or her, i.e. by taking legal proceedings for him or her to leave.

(4) The same as described under (3) can result from damage to furniture provided to your home, or, if you live in a flat, to common parts of the building, whether damaged by you, or someone living with you, with the same qualification concerning lodgers and sub-tenants.

(5) You got the tenancy by making a false statement. This may be a deliberately false statement, or a statement you weren't certain was false but that you made not caring whether or not it was true. (See also Chapter 1, in relation to application as homeless.)

(6) You got the tenancy by exchange (Chapter 3), and in connection with the exchange money was paid (whether to you, or by you). This can also apply if you have taken over the tenancy from a member of your family, who obtained the premises by an exchange, but only if that former tenant is still living with you.

(7) The tenancy was granted in connection with employment, and is of premises which are part of, or are in the grounds of, a non-housing building, and you or someone living in the property with you has been guilty of conduct such that it would not be right to let you remain. When deciding this question, the landlord and the court have to consider the purposes for which the "main" building is used: for example, petty theft by someone living in school grounds *might* not have this result, while violence or sexual offences probably will. It will depend initially on what the landlord thinks, and then on what a court thinks.

(8) As a secure tenant, you may be moved in order to allow works to be carried out on your home. You may be placed elsewhere by the landlord, and this temporary letting will probably be a secure tenancy in its own right.

If you moved on the understanding that you would go back once your former home was ready, you may be willing to return. On the other hand, if the time has been long, you have put down new roots, or you find the temporary place preferable, you may not wish to go back.

Once the former home is ready for you, if you are unwilling to return, the landlord can seek an order to make you do so. However, it still has to show that it is reasonable for you to return, because the court may well take your side, perhaps because it has taken much longer than originally planned, because of your children's schooling, or for some other reason.

Group 3

In relation to *this* group of "grounds" for making you leave, the landlord has to prove one of three sets of circumstances, *and*, in any of these three cases, that "suitable alternative accommodation" is available for you. It does *not* have to prove also that it is "reasonable" to make you move.

The key question, then, is what amounts to suitable alternative accommodation. It has to be accommodation itself let on a secure tenancy (see Chapter 2), or else on a fully protected private tenancy (although this will be rare).

See *The Private Tenant's Handbook* for details of full protection: note that if the tenancy is one which is fully protected in most respects but, by serving a notice on you at the outset of the tenancy, the landlord will at some future point have an absolute right to evict you (i.e. one not requiring him or her to show it is reasonable to evict you), it will *not* qualify as suitable alternative accommodation for this purpose.

The accommodation has to be reasonably suitable for your needs, and that of your family (but not necessarily of people living with you, such as lodgers or sub-tenants). When deciding whether or not the accommodation is reasonably suitable to your needs, the following must be taken into consideration:

(a) The usual sort of accommodation allocated by your landlord to people with needs similar to yours;

(b) distance from place of work or school or college, for you or members of your family;

(c) distance from the home of another member of your family, if you need or that other member needs to be close for their or your welfare (for example, in the case of an elderly or unwell relative);

(d) the amount and the cost of the accommodation offered (bearing in mind, however, that Housing Benefit – Chapter 9 – is likely to reduce cost if you cannot afford it yourself); note (see below) that in relation to the first of these "points" there is a special provision governing a move attributable to overcrowding;

(e) the terms on which the accommodation is to be made available (such as because it is only offered temporarily, or it is offered jointly with someone you do not wish to have a joint tenancy with), and the terms of the tenancy (see Chapter 6);

(f) if you have been provided with furniture hitherto, whether and what furniture is to be provided in the accommodation offered.

If your landlord is *not* a district council, London Borough Council or the Greater London Council, one of these councils may give your landlord a certificate stating that *it* will rehouse you, in which case there can be no argument about whether or not you will be getting suitable alternative accommodation. Their certificate is "final".

The three circumstances are:

(1) Your premises are overcrowded, to the extent that they are illegally overcrowded, i.e. you could be convicted of an overcrowding offence – this is described in detail in Chapter 4. In that chapter, two different ways of calculating overcrowding were described: one was based on whether people over the age of 10, not living together as husband and wife, *have* to sleep in the same room; the other was by reference to the number and sizes of rooms – this last is called the "room standard".

Extraordinarily, if the landlord moves you on account of illegal overcrowding at your *present* premises, the accommodation offered will be considered suitable *even if you would still be overcrowded under this "room standard"*.

(2) The second ground in relation to which the landlord need only prove that suitable alternative accommodation is available for you is that it is intending, within a reasonable time after getting the premises back from you, to demolish the premises, or reconstruct them, or carry out works to them, which it cannot reasonably do without evicting you.

One point may be made on this. If the premises are only being improved, and you do not wish to leave *permanently*, you can ask the landlord to rehouse you temporarily (reminding them that, all things being equal, if you later change your mind, they will probably be able to make you move back again: see (8) under Group 1).

The landlord does not have to agree: it may be that the premises will not be suitable for you after the works have been done (for instance, because there will be fewer rooms). Or, it may be administratively inconvenient. If they require you to move, you may be entitled to compensation (see Chapter 10).

In the first case – unsuitable after conversion – there will not be much you can do (except argue that what they have offered is not suitable). In the second case, you can argue to a court that if you are willing to move out *temporarily*, the authority do not need an order to move you *permanently*.

Whether or not this will succeed will depend on each case, and you will almost certainly need advice to launch this argument (see Chapter 12).

(3) If your landlord is a charity (which will not include local authorities or development corporations) with specific objects, and your continued occupation would conflict with those objects, you can be moved. This might happen if, for example the objects are for a purpose such as to help widows and widowers for a limited period after their partner's death.

This ground is similar to Group 4, ground (3) below. The important point of difference is that your landlord must be a charity, as that term is legally defined.

Group 4

In this group, the landlord has to prove that one out of five circumstances applies to you, *and* that it is reasonable to make the order, *and* that suitable alternative accommodation is available. Suitable alternative accommodation means the same as in Group 3. What is meant by reasonable is likely to be different, however, because we are not concerned here with anything you have done wrong, as we were under most of the grounds in Group 2.

More relevant will be how long you have lived in the premises, social ties such as friendships, clubs, societies, others who are dependent on you, schools for your children, religious centres, etc.

(1) The dwelling was in consequence of employment, and the premises are part of, or in the grounds of, a non-housing building, or a cemetery; no one in the employment for which the premises were let still lives in the house; and, the landlord needs the property for someone else to whom a job has been offered, and who has accepted (or has accepted conditional on accommodation being provided).

(2) The premises have features which make it suitable for occupation by a physically disabled person, there is no longer one such living in the property, and the landlord needs it for one such person.

(3) The landlord is a housing association (or trust) which lets housing to specific categories of people (see Chapter 2) with special needs (other than mere poverty) which make it difficult for those people to find their own housing; either there is no longer one such person living in the property or the local authority is offering to rehouse you under a secure tenancy; and the landlord needs the property for occupation by such a person.

One example of this is housing provided to women and their children who have fled their former homes on account of domestic violence or breakdown. Quite frequently, they are housed by an association, in circumstances which amount to secure tenancy but which are designed to give them the social or psychological support they will need at such a stressful time.

The idea is that, once they have settled down again, they can be moved into either local-authority accommodation or other accommodation owned by the landlord, and someone else with the same problem can use what is likely to be one of an all-too-small number of units.

(4) The property is one of a group, which the landlord lets to people with special needs, and a social services or other special facility is provided to help; there is no longer such a person in the property, and the landlord needs the property for one such person.

(5) The tenant has taken over on the death of a member of the family (other than a spouse). This ground was described earlier, in relation to succession on death (see Chapter 3).

Does the landlord have to get a court order to make me leave?

Yes. If the reason for your eviction is in Group 1 (see page 101), your right of occupation has become non-secure , in which case there is in one circumstance a theoretical possibility, described below, that no court order is necessary, but as a matter of practice a court order will always be sought.

No landlord can ever evict an occupier without at the least first bringing the right of occupation to an end. In the case of secure tenants, the *landlord* cannot bring the right of occupation to an end: it will always go on, until a *court* orders it to end, on one of the grounds described above.

This is true both of periodic tenancies and fixed-term tenancies (see Chapter 2). A fixed-term tenancy contains a date which is *said* to be its ending. If it is still secure at this date, then one of two things happens.

Either the landlord and the tenant *agree* a new *secure* fixed-term tenancy, *or* a periodic tenancy starts up *automatically*. Once that happens, the rules of periodic tenancy apply, which still, or again, means that the tenancy cannot be brought to an end, except by a court order on one of those grounds (see above).

How can the landlord get a court order to bring my secure tenancy to an end?

The procedure to be followed by the landlord is carefully prescribed. It is slightly different for those with periodic tenancies, and those with fixed-term tenancies (see Chapter 2).

A. Fixed-Term

A fixed-term tenancy comes to an end at a time which is specified – fixed – at the beginning of the tenancy. It can only be brought to an end beforehand *by the landlord* (see below for by the tenant) in one way.

That is, if the tenant breaks a term of the tenancy (see Chapter 6), the landlord can claim that the fixed-term tenancy has been *forfeit*. The landlord can only do this with a court order, and the court has power to grant the tenant what is called "relief from forfeiture", in effect overruling the forfeiture.

You have to ask the court for "relief", and the complexity of the law in this matter, which applies to non-secure fixed-term tenants as well as to fixed-term secure tenants, is such that advice and assistance is strongly recommended (see Chapter 12).

Before claiming forfeiture, on any ground other than non-payment of rent, the landlord must serve a preliminary notice, to give you an opportunity to rectify the breach of the term of your tenancy which it alleges.

If you do not rectify the breach within the time specified (which must be a reasonable time, or the court will not uphold it), or if the case is one of rent arrears, the landlord can proceed to court. It does this in the same way as for a periodic secure tenancy (see below), by issuing a notice, stating the grounds on which it intends to seek a court order.

When the matter comes before the court, the court will either grant relief from forfeiture or make an order. The order may mean eviction, by preventing or limiting the periodic tenancy which normally starts at the end of a fixed-term secure tenancy (see above), or you may find that you now have only the security of a periodic, rather than fixed-term, tenant.

The court will *automatically* grant relief from forfeiture in a rent arrears case if the arrears are cleared at least five days before the hearing.

B. Periodic

Non-secure tenancies are brought to an end by notice to quit. Secure tenancies are not brought to an end by notice to quit, but by court order.

There is a difference between notices or other proceedings which are just between the landlord and you, and those which are started in or through a court. Court proceedings are said to start when the landlord "issues" proceedings, which is not the same as when the landlord merely writes to, or serves a notice on, you.

The starting-point is a "notice of seeking possession", which the landlord serves, identifying the grounds on which it wishes to get you out. This notice has to be in the form prescribed by the government for this purpose.

The notice of seeking possession must state the *earliest* date on which the landlord can commence – i.e. issue – court proceedings.

This is more or less the same time as for a notice of variation of term of tenancy (see Chapter 6), i.e. four weeks, or a period of the tenancy (say, a full month), whichever is longer. (In the case of a yearly tenancy, only six months' is needed.) However, the date set must be one which is the first or the last day of a period of your tenancy (normally the day, or the day before, you are due the rent). This is the same as for "notice to quit" a non-secure tenancy (see below).

The notice of seeking possession is only in force for one year from that date, i.e. the earliest date the landlord can start the court proceedings. It follows that the notice of seeking possession normally lasts for one year and four weeks (because most periodic tenancies are weekly). If the landlord does not issue a court summons during the year it is in force, the notice simply lapses, and the landlord has to start again.

Once served with notice of seeking possession, you should not ignore it in the "hope that it will go away". Even if you hear nothing more for a while, this does not mean they have forgotten, just that they are taking their own time.

If the notice relates to some default, such as arrears or breach of term of tenancy, or nuisance, which you can rectify, you should do so, and write to the landlord saying that you have done so (keeping a copy of your letter). This may prevent the matter being taken further.

Otherwise, seek advice at the earliest possible time. It may be important for you to get legal help (see Chapter 12).

Even if the matter reaches court, it does not follow that an order will be made.

First of all, an order may be refused, because, for example, it is not reasonable to make it, the court is not satisfied that the circumstance described applies, or that suitable alternative accommodation will be available for you.

Even if the circumstances are made out, if the ground for possession is in Groups 2 or 4 (see above), the court may make a suspended or conditional order, i.e. letting you stay on terms, such as to clear the arrears, to put right damage to property or furniture, to stop being a nuisance to neighbours.

It will not normally do this in Group 4, although it may use the power to suspend to give you longer than if it were making an outright order, or else because the court wants the landlord to do something more (for example, decorate alternative accommodation), and to be satisfied that it has been done before the order will take effect.

If the court makes a suspended or conditional order, you will remain a secure tenant, unless or until you fail to comply with its terms.

If it makes an outright or absolute eviction order, which specifies that you have to leave at a certain date, you will cease to be a secure tenant on that date.

Even if an absolute order is made, you can reapply to the court if you think that there has been a change in circumstances, sufficient to make the court change its mind, such as that you now have money with which to clear arrears. You must do this before the date set for you to leave.

If a suspended or conditional order has been made, then when you have complied with the conditions – for example, cleared the arrears, or if a lengthy time has passed without having caused any further nuisance – you can also reapply, to revoke the order.

If the case is one of arrears, you should take the trouble to do this, because otherwise the landlord may seek to use the old order if you fall into arrears again at a later time.

If I have to go, how much time will the court give me?

In those cases where the court has power to grant a suspended or conditional order (Groups 2 and 4), the court has a discretion to give you as long as it thinks fit.

In other cases, you will get only from two to six weeks, depending on the hardship the eviction will cause, and you will be obliged during the time allowed to pay current rent, and if there are arrears, probably also money off the arrears.

Can I end the tenancy myself?

A. Fixed Term

In the case of a fixed-term secure tenancy, you can only "surrender" it if *either* the agreement itself makes provision for you to give notice – for example, at specific times ("break-clauses") – *or* the landlord agrees to your giving up. Merely quitting will still leave you liable for the premises, including rent.

If the fixed-term is a joint tenancy, you *all* need to agree to bring it to an end, in either of the ways described, i.e. if one of you wants to stay, the other cannot bring it to an end alone. In this case, unless the landlord agrees to substitute a tenancy in the one who stays, even if you are the one to go you will remain one of the joint tenants. As such, you will still be liable on the terms of the tenancy, such as for rent, other charges, damage, etc. However, you will have a right of action against the (remaining) tenant.

B. Periodic

If the tenancy is periodic, you can give formal notice to quit to the landlord, at any time, and without any special reason. This is a notice in writing which identifies who you are, who the landlord is, what the premises are, and the date when you intend to quit.

That date must be of the same length as for variation of term of tenancy (see Chapter 6), i.e. four weeks or one period of tenancy, whichever is the longer. Also, you must state the date as the first or the last day of a period of your tenancy: for example, the last day before your next rent day.

If you are in any doubt about exactly what day of the week, or month, your tenancy runs from, add the words "or the last day of my tenancy expiring next four weeks (or one month) after the service of this notice upon you." This is called a "saving clause," and it throws the burden on to the landlord to work out the exact date.

This formality of notice is not necessary if your agreement is one of *licence* (see Chapter 2). You must still let the landlord know you are going, which is best done in writing, and you must give reasonable warning, which is probably no more than a week or two. However, you do not need to worry about these precise dates.

Do not just "quit". You will remain liable for the premises, including the rent, at least until the landlord (a) finds out you have gone, and (b) agrees to accept your departure, i.e. to treat the tenancy as at an end.

If the tenancy is a joint tenancy, then in contrast to the position with fixed-term tenancies it only needs one of you to serve notice to quit, whether or not the other agrees.

You should not serve notice to quit unless you have somewhere else to go to, or on advice (see comments on quitting because of rent rise in Chapter 6, and on intentional homelessness in Chapter 1).

You should not serve notice to quit, as one of the joint tenants, just because you want to go, because you may deprive the other person of his or her home too. Instead, seek agreement from the landlord for you to go and the other to remain as the only tenant, or from the other tenant that he or she will (in writing, if you wish) promise to be responsible for the premises, including the rent.

What happens to people living with a secure tenant when the secure tenant quits or is ordered to go?

Normally, their rights of occupation come to an end at the same time as those of the secure tenant. There is one circumstance – when the secure tenant *gives* notice to quit, or "surrenders" (see page 98) – when a *sub-tenant* may be said to have become the landlord's tenant; this is described in *The Private Tenant's Handbook*, along with the other rights of occupiers as against *their* landlord, i.e. the secure tenant himself or herself.

Non-secure occupiers

What security of tenure do I have as a non-secure occupier?

With one exception, you have no greater security of tenure than the agreement allows. If it is a fixed-term tenancy or licence (see Chapter 2), then you will have as long as has been agreed, unless you break one of the terms of the agreement, in which case the landlord can try to bring the agreement to an end.

In the case of a fixed-term *tenancy*, this will mean that the tenancy has to be *forfeit* by the landlord.

The provisions peculiar to forfeiture described above in relation to secure tenancies – i.e. preliminary notice giving you an opportunity to rectify breach, other than where the case is one of arrears, and the right to ask for "relief" – apply in this case as well. If arrears are paid off five days before the hearing, relief is automatic.

In the case of a periodic tenancy or licence, the landlord can bring the agreement to an end at any time, and whether or not there has been any breach by you.

If the landlord is a local authority or a development corporation, and can be shown to be acting wholly outrageously, you *may* be able to do something in law to stop the proceedings, but this will certainly need advice and assistance (see Chapter 12).

Otherwise, all the landlord has to do is to give you notice. If the agreement is one of licence, this does not have to be in writing, and need only be for a "reasonable" period, which will depend on such factors as how long you have lived there, and also why you are being asked to go – for example, because you have behaved badly.

The one exception to this rule is if the licence itself specified that a minimum period of notice will be given. In this case, the landlord must give at least that much notice, or a reasonable period, whichever is the *longer*.

If the agreement is one of *tenancy*, then you must be given a formal written notice to quit which meets all the conditions described in relation to a secure tenant's notice *to* his or her landlord (i.e. four weeks or one period of tenancy whichever is the longer, expiring on first or last day of period of tenancy, identifying landlord, tenant and premises).

In addition, the notice must inform you that:

"If the tenant does not leave the dwelling, the landlord must get an order for possession from the court before the tenant can lawfully be evicted. The landlord cannot apply for such an order before the notice to quit has run out.

"A tenant who does not know if he has any right to remain in possession after a notice to quit runs out, or is otherwise unsure of his rights, can obtain advice from a solicitor. Help with all or part of the cost of legal advice and assistance may be available under the Legal Aid Scheme. He should also be able to obtain information from a Citizens' Advice Bureau, a Housing Aid Centre, a Rent Officer or Rent Tribunal Office." (See also Chapter 12.)

If the notice to quit does not contain this information, or does not comply with the other technical conditions described, it is "invalid", i.e. as if it had not been served. In this case, the tenancy has not been brought to an end at all. However, before deciding to treat a notice as invalid, take advice (see Chapter 12).

The one exception to this complete lack of security is the *periodic licence* which qualifies as a "restricted contract" (see Chapter 2), *and* which began before 28 November 1980. This class of occupier can get security from the Rent Tribunal, which defers the ending of the agreement.

This is basically a private-sector right, which a few people in the public sector (those described as such in Chapter 2) happen to benefit from. The right, and how it is exercised, is described in *The Private Tenant's Handbook.*

Does the landlord have to get a court order to evict me?

As a matter of practice, all the public landlords *will* get a court order before evicting people.

They always *have* to get one against a former tenant. If you have been a non-secure *licensee,* they do not *have* to get a court order to evict you except in one case. In all cases, however, the agreement must have come to an end, before they can get a court order.

The one exception, where they cannot evict a former licensee without a court order, is that class of licensee described in Chapter 2 as occupying under a ''restricted contract'', whose contract began on or after 28 November 1980, i.e. this is *instead* of the right to go to the Rent Tribunal (see above).

How long can the court give me?

Not long. Except for those who have been occupying under ''restricted contracts'' which started on or after 28 November 1980 (see above), it is normally two weeks, unless you can show that there will be exceptional hardship, in which case the maximum is six weeks (and on terms that you pay current rent, and probably also money off arrears).

In the case of a person who has had a restricted contract which started on or after 28 November 1980, the court can give you up to a maximum of three months.

Can I bring the agreement to an end myself?

Yes. The rules are exactly the same as in relation to secure tenants (see page 98).

8: Rent and Other Charges

What will I have to pay to live in the premises?

You will have to pay what it is agreed under the right of occupation, as charges to be met by you. This will almost invariably include rent (although under an employment arrangement, this may be deducted from your wages, or else you may be paid less but receive free accommodation).

Whether or not you also have to pay rates depends on whether or not rates have been included in your rent. Rents may be *inclusive* of rates, in which case the rates are treated as part of the rent; or, they may be *exclusive*, in which case you may either be responsible for paying them directly to the rating authority, or you may pay them to the landlord, but as a sum separately identified.

You may also have to pay a service charge, but this will normally only occur in blocks of flats. A service charge covers repairs, maintenance, insurance or management, and any other special "services" or "facilities". These may be charged separately from the rent, because their cost is unpredictable.

You may also be linked up to a "district heating system", under which some or all of your heating is provided from a central source, and you are charged either at a fixed rate or at a rate which reflects the amount of heating you use.

You will normally also have to pay for gas and electricity yourself, i.e. directly. In a hostel, for example, or a house in which you occupy no more than a single room, however, these costs may either be included in the rent, or charged for by meter. In the latter case, it will be your landlord who decides how much gas or electricity you get for your money, but there are legal limits on how much "profit" they can make, to cover the costs of the meter and collection from it.

Public landlords are unlikely to overcharge except by accident. If in doubt, check with the local gas or electricity board. Because this will be rare where public landlords are concerned, it will not be described further here.

In addition to these charges, two related matters can conveniently be mentioned in this chapter: the right tp a rent book; and, how rent and other charges may be recovered.

We are *not* concerned here with how you can get help to meet any or all of these charges. That is the subject of Chapter 9: Housing Benefits.

Rent

How is rent fixed?

There are two "systems" for fixing rents, which apply to the public landlords (see Chapter 2) considered in this book. First, there is the system that is really not a system at all, and which applies to local authorities, and development corporations: the landlord decides!

Secondly, there is the system – properly described as such – which applies to the tenants of housing associations.

In each case, what is described applies equally to secure tenants and to non-secure occupiers, although there will be differences when it comes to varying (which normally means increasing) the rent of a non-secure occupier whose landlord is a local authority or development corporation.

A. Local Authority/Development Corporation

How do local authorities/development corporations decide the levels of rents?

These landlords have a discretion to decide what rents they want to charge. Authorities have a legal duty to charge a *reasonable* rent, but it is for them to decide what is "reasonable". This can vary from something close to what the premises cost to provide, to a low, subsidised rent.

Local authorities receive public subsidies for their housing functions. What they receive depends in part on their rental income. However, the government provides subsidy not on what rental income the authority actually receives, but on what the government thinks they ought to receive.

In this way, government brings pressure to bear on local authorities to charge higher rents than many of them would wish to do.

In theory, you can challenge a decision to increase rents – because you think that what is being charged is unreasonably high, for example. (Local ratepayers can also challenge a local authority – not a development corporation – because they think the rents are unreasonably low!)

In practice, this is extremely unlikely to succeed, and you would certainly need legal advice and assistance (see Chapter 12), and be *well-advised* to co-ordinate or co-operate with other tenants, through, for instance, a tenants' association or organisation (see Chapter 11).

Will the rent be inclusive or exclusive of rates?

This will depend on the agreement. As a rule of thumb, if you have a self-contained home, whether house or flat, the rent is likely to be exclusive of rates, but whether or not you have to pay the rates to the landlord or directly to the rating authority (which may be the landlord, wearing another hat) will vary from locality to locality.

If, on the other hand, you live in a hostel, you will certainly be paying a rent inclusive of rates, and if you occupy no more than a single room, albeit not in a hostel, you are highly likely to be paying rent inclusive.

Will the rent include the cost of services?

It may do, or it may not. It depends entirely on what the agreement says. If a right to an additional charge for services is reserved under the agreement, the service charge will be additional to the rent; otherwise, it will not.

An additional, variable service charge is not common where the landlord is a local authority or development corporation. If there *is* such a charge, there are provisions (aimed mainly at the private sector) which enable you to make sure you are being charged no more than is reasonable, and for a reasonable standard of work (see *The Private Tenant's Handbook*).

Will the rent include heating?

If some or all the heating is provided by the landlord, then either the cost will be included in the rent, or there will be an additional charge, which may be of a fixed amount, or may be variable, calculated according to how much heating you use. It depends entirely on what the agreement says. (See further below.)

How can the landlord increase the rent?

The position depends on two features: whether or not you are a secure tenant, and whether or not you have a periodic or fixed-term agreement (see Chapter 2).

(1) *Secure Tenant – Periodic.* Unless the agreement contains a provision enabling the landlord to increase the rent (which is uncommon, but could happen with, for example, a service or heating charge), rent can only be changed by notice of variation, in the way described in Chapter 6. Note that no prior consultation notice has to be served.

(2) *Secure Tenant – Fixed-Term.* This was also described in Chapter 6. If the agreement makes provision for increase, such as for service or heating charge, or otherwise, then the manner of increasing the rent is that which is set out in the agreement. Such clauses are now not uncommon in fixed-term agreements.

Otherwise, it is part of the purpose of a fixed-term agreement that you should know the exact terms on which you will occupy, for a fixed period of time, and accordingly the rent cannot be increased.

The landlord therefore has to wait until the term comes to an end, when a new term may be negotiated – doubtless at an increased rent, – or a periodic tenancy automatically comes into force, when the rules for periodic tenancies will apply.

(3) *Non-Secure – Periodic.* The position depends both in practice and in law on whether your agreement is tenancy or licence (see Chapter 2).

If a licence, then unless *either* the agreement contains a clause permitting the landlord to increase the rent (which is uncommon), *or* you agree to the variation, the landlord can only increase the rent by determining the right of occupation, i.e. by notice, which must be of a reasonable period, or the minimum period stated in the agreement, whichever is the *longer* (see Chapter 7).

The landlord may well invite you to agree the variation, because less formality attaches to a licence than a tenancy. If you want to stay on, you have little practical choice but to agree, because of the ease with which your agreement can be brought to an end (see Chapter 7).

If the agreement is one of *tenancy*, then there are a number of ways the variation can take place. First of all, although this is uncommon, the agreement may provide for increase, in which case the landlord need only stick to whatever provisions (minimum time, warning, etc.) the agreement requires. This may be the case for a service or heating charge.

Secondly, the landlord can invite you to agree the change. This will be rare, because there is more formality in tenancy, and from an administrative or bureaucratic perspective, the landlord will be reluctant to put the change through other than with maximum formality.

Thirdly, there is a notice of variation procedure, more or less the same as that applicable to secure tenants (see Chapter 6). However, although this procedure has been available since 1968, public landlords have rarely used it.

Finally, and most commonly of all, the landlord will serve notice to quit (see Chapter 7), but – assuming all it wants is a rent increase – grant a new tenancy, at a higher rent.

B. Housing Associations

How are housing assocation rents decided?

The position is different for tenancies and licences (see Chapter 2).

(1) *Licences.* Rents for licences are decided by the landlord, and with one exception, there can be no challenge to what they decide. Some licensees may, however, have "restricted contracts" (see Chapter 2). A licensee with a restricted contract can ask an independent tribunal called the Rent Tribunal to fix a "reasonable" rent for the premises. This is really a private-sector right, and details of how this can be done will be found in *The Private Tenant's Handbook.*

(2) *Tenancies.* This is what most housing association rights of occupation will be. Their rents are the same as those charged in the private sector. They are called "fair rents", and they are fixed by independent officials called Rent Officers (and, on appeal, an independent tribunal called the Rent Assessment Committee).

A detailed description of the "fair rent system" will be found in *The Private Tenant's Handbook.* What follows is an outline, concentrating on the aspects most likely to be of interest to the housing-association (as distinct from the private) tenant.

"Fair rents" are rents which the Rent Officer decides – "registers" – as the right rent for the premises, ignoring *both* the general scarcity of accommodation *and* any personal circumstances of either landlord or tenant.

Thus, the fact that the landlord is a public body will be ignored, as will, for example, the fact that the property may be a flat at the top of a lot of stairs and the tenant is elderly, or, the fact that there is no garden and the tenant is particularly keen on gardening.

That does not mean that stairs or garden are ignored: just that the value or detriment to the particular tenant is ignored. They will be counted along with the other factors which help to determine rents: location, size, condition of property, local and internal facilities, terms of tenancy, furniture (if any), etc.

The *best* indication of what a fair rent is likely to be will be a rent that has been registered for other similar premises. These may be privately-owned premises, although if what you live in has been recently built you will find that most similar premises are others owned by housing associations.

Similar rents are known as "comparables". If trying to decide whether what is proposed or has been registered for your premises is fair, by referring to comparables, be sure to note when they were registered, because rents usually increase with time (inflation). Also note particular features, such as condition of property.

You can see "comparables" on the Rent Register, which is maintained by the Rent Officer. Some records will note that a rent was appealed to, and accordingly fixed or confirmed by the Rent Assessment Committee, and these rents are of more influence than those fixed by a Rent Officer.

You will not normally need to know *how* to get a fair rent registered, because your landlord is likely to make the application, and cannot then charge you a rent higher than has been fixed by a Rent Officer.

Sometimes, housing associations get provisional rents fixed, *before* a letting, for example before property is built or converted into flats. They then charge this provisional rent until the rent is confirmed: the rent should and can be adjusted later.

If, as is unlikely, the landlord has *not* arranged for a rent registration, you will have to pay the rent set at the beginning of your tenancy *until* a registered rent is organised. If *you* wish to arrange this, you should seek advice (Chapter 12) on how to go about it (and whether it is worthwhile).

Whenever the rent is registered by a Rent Officer, or indeed on appeal by a Rent Assessment Committee, you will always have the opportunity to make representations, and there will normally be a visit to the premises. Use the opportunity to draw attention to any drawbacks of living in the premises: hidden disrepair, lack of facilities, inconsiderate design aspects, and so on.

Once a rent has been registered, it will fix for two years, and there will have to be a new application before an increase can be registered. As rents will normally increase, you do not not want to apply for an increase but will want to wait for the landlord to get round to it. The more it delays, the better it suits you.

There can be a variation, in one circumstance, in less than two years. That is, if there is some material change, such as the installation of a new facility or a major improvement. It is in this case the landlord which will want the re-application, to secure an increase.

Theoretically, you could apply for a *decrease* during the two years, on account of some deterioration. However, on a "mid-term application", the Rent Officer reconsiders the rent as a whole, and does not just, say, knock something off, or add something on.

As, therefore, inflation is likely to have caused an overall increase, you would be unlikely to benefit from a mid-term application, complaining of deterioration, unless it is very major indeed, in which case, having regard to Chapter 10, you are likely to be taking advice in any event and can raise this point with your adviser.

Your point of interest is whether or not to appeal the rent fixed, to a Rent Assessment Committee. When notified of the Rent Officer's decision, you will also be told of your right to appeal, and how to exercise it. (It requires no more than a letter, within twenty-eight days, asking for the matter to be referred to the Committee.)

Rent Assessment Committees *tend* to *increase* rents, rather than reduce them, and they have the right to do this, even if it is your appeal. Only if the Rent Officer's increase seems very high, either in comparison to a former rent fixed (if any) or to other rents, should you contemplate appeal.

It is well worth taking advice (Chapter 12), or consulting and comparing notes with a tenants' association (if any), or other tenants' organisation (Chapter 11).

Will the rent be inclusive of rates?

(1) Licences: if you occupy a hostel, or a single room in a house, with shared facilities, you will probably have no more than a licence, and your rent will almost certainly be inclusive of rates. If you occupy "short-life property" (see Chapter 2), you may also have a licence, and the arrangement is likely to be one under which you pay your rates direct to the rating authority (see below).

(2) If you are a tenant, your rent will normally be exclusive of rates, which may either be paid direct to the rating authority, or be collected by the landlord as an addition to the rent, depending on what has been arranged.

The rent fixed (see above) by the Rent Officer will be a rent *exclusive* of rates. The landlord is entitled to add the rates to the rent fixed, even if you do pay an inclusive rent.

Will the rent include services?

(1) Licences: the rent will usually include any additional charges, such as for services.

(2) Tenancies: if you live in a block of flats, or occasionally even in a house on an estate, there may be an additional charge, for services.

If the rent is fixed by the Rent Officer or Rent Assessment Committee, it will be decided – and recorded – how much of your rent is attributable to services provided to you.

It will also be decided – and recorded – whether the amount payable for service ought to be a fixed part of the rent or whether it can be an additional and variable amount. The landlord will only be granted permission to enjoy the benefit of a variable amount if the *way* in which the variation is to be calculated is *reasonable*.

In the case of a flat, this is likely to be so, because the provisions referred to above and which are mainly aimed at the private sector, which ensure that you do not have to pay more than a reasonable amount, will apply (see *The Private Tenant's Handbook)*.

Otherwise, such as in the case of a house on an estate to which services are provided, it depends on the terms of the agreement, i.e. how the agreement states that variation is to be calculated. The amount will not normally be allowed to be varied if relatively few services are provided, so that their value does not amount to a significant part of the whole rent – for example, if these services are worth less than 5 per cent of the rent.

Will the rent include heating?

(1) Licences: rents under licences, in hostels and single rooms, commonly include heating, and the charge is part of the rent. In short-life property, heating is almost certain *not* to be provided, nor, of course to be charged for.

(2) Tenancies: heating may be provided, and either charged as part of the rent or as an addition.

Where the rent is fixed by the Rent Officer, heating is treated as a "service", and therefore it is a matter for the Rent Officer (or Assessment Committee) whether the landlord ought to be permitted to charge a variable amount. (See also below.)

How can the landlord increase the rent?

(1) Licences: the position of the licensee of a housing association is the same as that of a non-secure licensee of a local authority or development corporation (see page 106), except in the case of a licensee with a restricted contract.

If a rent has been decided by the Rent Tribunal, it cannot be increased without their approval. As it is the landlord who will want the increase, not you, you do not need to know how the application is made, although you will, of course, have an opportunity to present your arguments as to what the rent ought to be.

The increase will not take effect until you are served with a notice of the Tribunal's decision.

Technically, and with one exception, unless the licence permits increase (as with non-secure licensees – see above), you can refuse to pay the increase unless and until the landlord brings the licence to an end, and grants a new one. However, as you will have so little security (see Chapter 7), you are not well-advised to refuse unless you are also willing to quit.

The one exception is if your initial agreement was for a level of rent which the Rent Tribunal has later *reduced*, and the new rent fixed by the Tribunal is *still* less than originally agreed. In this circumstance, the landlord has a right, even under the contract, and therefore without bringing it to an end, to the increase.

(2) Tenancies: the increase will normally be on a new decision of the Rent Officer, i.e. after two years (see page 109). It could also be from a rent fixed by the Rent Officer, which has been appealed to the Rent Assessment Committee.

In the case of a periodic tenancy, except in the case of a variable service charge, the rent increase cannot be earlier than the date of (either class of) decision, nor can it take effect until the landlord has served notice of variation (which has to fulfil the same requirements as a notice of variation of any other term: see Chapter 6).

In the case of a fixed-term tenancy (which will be uncommon from a housing association), then unless the agreement permits increases, such as for services, the landlord *cannot* raise the rent beyond the limit set out in the agreement, unless and until the agreement comes to an end (when if the tenancy is secure, there will either be a new agreement, or a periodic tenancy: see Chapter 7).

Whether under a periodic or fixed-term agreement, however, the full increase will not be passed on at once, *unless* it is an increase by a Rent Assessment Committee over a decision of the Rent Officer.

In other cases, only half the "rent" increase will be passed on in the first year, and the other half in the second year. This is called "phasing". However, the "rent" which qualifies for "phasing" is the "pure" rent, not including rates, or any amount attributed to heating or services (whether or not a "variable" service element: see above).

Rates

What are rates?

Rates are payments required by the local authority, which depend on the rateable value of the premises you occupy: local authorities decide annually how much rates they will charge "in the pound". This means that they may decide to charge 50p in the pound, so that if you have a house with a rateable value of £300, your rates for that year will be £150. The authority can even charge more than one-for-one: they can decide to levy rates at an amount of, for example, £1.50 per pound, so that, in this example, the rates will be £450 for the year.

To whom will I pay my rates?

This will depend on your agreement. There are two broad possibilities: either you pay your rates to the local authority directly or you will pay them to your landlord, who passes them on to the authority.

Will my premises be separately rated?

If you are the tenant or the licensee of a whole house, your premises will certainly be separately rated. If you are the tenant or licensee of a self-contained flat, they are likely to be. If you are the tenant or licensee of a single room, or rooms in a flat which is not self-contained, they are unlikely to be separately rated.

How can I find out whether my premises are separately rated?

You can find this out by asking the local authority for your area (who may also be your landlord; the rates will, however, normally be handled by a different department).

What will it mean if my premises are not separately rated?

In this case, you will certainly be paying your rates to your landlord, because without separate rating there can be no separate or direct rate demand from you.

If I pay rates to the landlord, can it pass increases on to me?

This will depend on whether your rent is inclusive or exclusive. If it is exclusive, yes. If it is inclusive, the rates can only be passed on as and when and how the rent can be increased (see page 105).

In the case of a fair-rented housing association property, there does not need to be a new registration, but there will still need to be a notice of variation.

Heating Charges

What are heating charges?

Heating charges are charges made for heating provided by the landlord. This does not mean the provision of heating *systems*, or *installations*, but power to and through heating systems or installations (i.e. ''actual'' heating).

When will I have to pay a heating charge?

If you are provided with actual heating by the landlord, you are likely to have to pay for it. This may be done by the identification of a fixed element in your rent as a heating charge, or else you may have an element in your rent which is ''on account'' of heating, coupled to a requirement to pay a balance at the end of a period (usually a year) related to what you actually use.

At present, there are only two ways in which you can challenge the heating element in your rent. First of all, if you pay a variable amount, and live in a flat, you are within the service charge provisions referred to above, and described in *The Private Tenant's Handbook*: heating is a ''service'' for this purpose. Otherwise, the only challenge can be on the ground that you are simply not being provided with what you are paying for, or that you are not being charged according to the terms of the contract. In effect, you are either saying that the landlord is in breach of contract (non-provision) or that the landlord has no right in law to recover the money claimed (not in accordance with terms).

Both of these are difficult exercises. If you know of no one else with the same problem, you will need advice and assistance (see Chapter 12). However, as heating systems operate in blocks, across estates, or across districts, it is extremely unlikely that only you are affected, and you should contact the local tenants' association (if any) or other tenants' organisation (see Chapter 11).

The government have recently introduced *power* to draw up a scheme which would permit *secure* tenants to challenge heating charges, in a way similar to that which can be used to challenge service charges (see page 105). This scheme has *not* been put into effect, and you would accordingly be wrong to *assume* you have you have such a right, other than in the two ways described.

Rent Books

Am I entitled to a rent book?

If under your right of occupation you are to pay your rent weekly, you will be entitled to be provided by the landlord with a rent book, or some other similar such document (such as a rent card): this applies whether you are a secure tenant or a non-secure occupier.

The one exception to this is if the rent includes payment for board, and the value of the board forms a substantial part of the whole rent paid: this is a formula used in defining certain licensees who are excluded from having restricted contracts, because of the provision of board (see Chapter 2).

Rent books, or other similar documents, have to contain certain information: name and address of landlord and information prescribed by the government. The information prescribed includes particulars as to rent, terms of contracts and rights such as those to share facilities. In addition, the rent book must contain details of the overcrowding laws (see Chapter 4).

The failure to provide you with a rent book does not permit you to withhold the rent.

Recovery of Rent

If I do not pay the rent, will I be evicted?

Non-payment of rent is one of the grounds for possession against secure tenants (see Chapter 7) and is likely to be a reason for the landlord bringing to an end a non-secure right of occupation (for which, generally, it needs no specific reason: see Chapter 7).

Of course, if you are a secure tenant, arrears will not *necessarily* lead to an outright eviction order (see Chapter 7), although the proceedings will be in the form of eviction proceedings, and the threat of eviction is used to try and pressure you to pay.

The landlord does not *have* to use eviction proceedings to regain the rent. It can also use a direct rent action.

In addition, some public landlords – and, in particular, some local authorities – use a very old-fashioned method of recovering their rent, namely, "distress". What this means is that they seize your property and, if you do not pay the debt immediately, exercise the right to sell it off, which usually means at substantially less than it cost, or would cost to replace. This is a vicious way to recover rent, because it worsens the poverty of those already in financial difficulty. It is, quite literally, a medieval remedy.

Distress is governed by rules of technicality unparalleled by anything in this book, developed by judges over the last few hundred years. There are limits on when distress can take place, how it can be carried out, and what sort of property can be taken (items not to be removed include some clothing and bedding, work tools, perishable food, things in actual use, etc.). If the landlord is threatening you with distress, you should take *immediate* advice as to how to stop them or, if they have already started to do it, how to prevent them going any further (see Chapter 12).

9: Housing Benefits

What are housing benefits?

Housing benefits are government-funded, means-tested welfare benefits which help people meet a range of their housing costs. The housing benefit scheme is administered by local authorities, i.e. district councils and London Borough councils.

The *details* of housing benefit are not only complicated but also frequently change, and in a guide like this there is danger in being too specific. A statement that this amount is or is not available, or that benefit starts when you have this or that amount of income, might have the effect of discouraging you from applying. Instead of describing the scheme in any detail, therefore, I shall only indicate in outline its *main* points or principles, as a guide to how to go about getting benefit and what to look out for. Even so, there can be frequent changes, in even those main points or principles, and you should therefore always check.

Can I claim housing benefit?

Yes. Whether or not you will *qualify* for benefit, and for how much, will depend on a range of factors considered below. But any occupier can *claim* the benefit, whether you are the occupier of a whole house, of a flat, of a room, or whether you live in a hostel or share accommodation with someone else. You can also apply if you are in full-time work, or even if you have money saved up.

When you claim benefit, the authority will define what is called your "assessment unit", i.e. family or household. Only *one* person from each assessment unit can claim and receive housing benefit (but the other people are of course taken into account when deciding how much: see below).

The assessment unit includes you, your partner if any (whether or not legally married), any "dependent children", and anyone else living in the property *as a member of the household* (i.e. not a sub-tenant). A lodger or boarder who makes payment including for food you provide may be treated as part of your assessment unit, or may claim benefit in his or her own right.

Dependent children means any child below 16 years of age or a child between 16 and 20 who is (a) still in full-time education, and (b) in respect of whom Child Benefit (another welfare benefit) is payable. Non-dependants are other members of the household, for instance, an adult son or daughter, or an elderly relative).

There has to be some degree of permanence, in order to show that what is being paid for is for somewhere to live *as a home:* you will not be entitled to housing benefit while renting a cottage in the country for a holiday.

If you live in a hostel, you *may* have to "establish" residence by a fourteen-day delay. (You will *not* have to do this if you receive supplementary benefit – see below – or if the authority is already satisfied that you occupy the hostel as a home. If the authority makes you wait, you should still make the claim because once you have established residence, your benefit will be backdated).

Students, too, can claim. However, the rules for assessing how much benefit is payable are different and take into account the "accommodation element" in their grants.

Normally, the claimant is the person who in law is responsible for the rent. Even if the tenancy or licence agreement is in another name, however, someone else who pays the rent may claim – for example if a tenant goes abroad for a period of months and allows you to live in his or her home, or else where one partner in a relationship is "the tenant" (or licensee) but the other partner actually pays (perhaps, but not necessarily, because the tenant has left).

Where there are joint tenants, the *normal* principle is to apportion the rent between them, and each is then assessed as liable for just that part. This does *not* apply to a married couple or a couple living together as husband and wife. In these cases, one is treated as the "principal" earner, or "head of the household", and considered liable for the whole rent, with the other taken into account as a member of the family. (Rules have recently been introduced to prevent this being used – as it could otherwise have been used – as a way of increasing entitlement artificially.)

Benefit is normally only available for one home at a time. There are two circumstances when it may be available for more.

First, if one person is liable to pay rent, but has fled the home because of domestic violence. Thus, for example, a woman tenant of one property leaves because of domestic violence and finds a new home elsewhere: she will then be liable for rent on both properties. It may be, perhaps because she has left the children or some of the children behind, that she does not want to stop paying the rent, and see her former partner, and the children, thrown on to the streets, at least until matters have been sorted out on a more permanent basis.

Secondly, but to a maximum of four weeks, when someone moves home and has to pay rent on two properties at once: for example, if the new home has to be taken at once but the move cannot take place, either because the new home is not ready for occupation or because of some other delay, such as waiting for school term to end or for a period of notice at an old job to run out.

Benefit may continue to be claimed during a period of absence, for instance while an in-patient in hospital, during a temporary stay in local authority residential accommodation, while looking for work elsewhere, on holiday or during a short term of imprisonment.

What payments qualify for benefit?

Housing benefit is available for rent, rates (but not water rates, or arrears of general rates). Rates are included whether you pay an inclusive or exclusive rent (see Chapter 8). Only the rates applicable to the part of the property occupied *as a home* will qualify, such as in a case where a house is used partly as a home and partly as a shop, or for a business.

It is possible that less than the whole rent will qualify if the rent includes payment for "non-qualifying services". In this case, even if your agreement does not apportion the costs, the authority will do so.

Non-qualifying services are: payments for lighting, heating (normally, but see below) and window cleaning of *premises* (see below on common parts), sports facilities (for instance, attached to an estate), laundering of personal items, charges for cooking or for hot water, and board.

Qualifying *if* the service is necessary and reasonable, and you are obliged to pay for them under the terms of your agreement (i.e. not if they are optional extras), are: furniture, services related to gardens, children's play areas, access (such as lifts), common parts (including their lighting, heating and window cleaning), entryphones, caretaking, rubbish collection, garaging/parking charges, radio or television aerial or relay service, and warden or other special services for the elderly or disabled.

There is no *maximum* rent which qualifies, per person or per household. If a rent is *registered* with the Rent Officer (housing association tenants) or the Rent Tribunal (restricted contracts) – see Chapter 8 – that rent is the maximum amount which will qualify for benefit. Otherwise, it is normally the full rent which is payable which qualifies, subject to the non-qualifying items considered in the last few paragraphs.

There is provision, however, for an authority to decide that a lower rent ought to qualify, if they consider the accommodation occupied unreasonably large, or unreasonably expensive, or in an unreasonably expensive area. This is unlikely to apply (although not impossible) in the public sector.

If you have a sub-tenant, or there are non-dependent (see above) members of your household, your rent will be notionally reduced, to allow for notional or actual "rents" paid by them to you.

If there is a sub-tenant, your rent may be reduced by the amount actually received, *less* any part attributable to water rates, heating and lighting, furniture, other services or the provision by you of board. In effect, your expenses are to be knocked off your sub-tenant's rent, so that only your "profit" is taken into account.

For non-dependent members of your household, fixed deductions are made. No non-dependant is taken into account, who is in full-time education and for whose requirement you provide, wholly or in part, and only one deduction is made if you have two non-dependants living with you as a couple, i.e. as husband and wife.

The rates of the fixed deduction depend on age, and other factors.

If either you or your partner is *blind*, no deduction should be made on account of a non-dependant; the same may be true if the non-dependant is a person providing residential assistance (i.e. care) to you or your partner.

No deduction should be made for a non-dependant who normally lives somewhere else.

In the case of someone living in a hostel, only the accommodation element of their payments will be met. If board is provided, and they qualify as a "certificated case" (see below), they will not receive housing benefit at all, but Supplementary Benefit instead.

How much benefit will I get?

How much you will actually get depends not only on your qualifying payments, but also on your income and other factors.

The question has to be considered separately for three classes: (a) if you receive Supplementary Benefit ("certificated cases"); (b) if you do not ("standard cases"); and (c) a special class known as "worse-off" cases (i.e. the availability of housing benefit may prevent you qualifying for Supplementary Benefit where you would otherwise qualify, and leaves you "worse off". This category exists in order to put you back in the position you would have been in).

A. Certificated Cases

If you qualify for Supplementary Benefit you ought to receive 100 per cent of the eligible housing costs, i.e. less deductions described above, such as board, heating, some service charges, water rates (which are intended to be met out of the Supplementary Benefit itself), sub-tenants, non-dependants.

Not all of the cost of heating, or other "fuel" charges, such as hot water, cooking and lighting, will be deducted, however, if you have to pay a fixed charge, as part of the terms of your tenancy, and where you do not have any control over the cost (unlike in the case of a variable charge, based on what you actually use – see Chapter 8).

In this case, there are amounts specified for each of the items mentioned, which are added together. If what you have to pay is *more* than the amount specified for the purpose of Housing Benefit, you will get an additional amount of benefit. If what you have to pay under your right of occupation is the same or less, however, it is still deducted.

This addition applies *only* if what you are provided with is full heating, lighting, hot water or cooking. If all you are provided with for the fixed charge (for example "background" heating) is only *part* of what you need, the addition should be *increased*, or, put another way, a *lower* specified sum should be taken into account.

Thus, if you pay a fixed charge for 100 per cent heating, it will be compared to 100 per cent of the specified sum, and you will get nothing if the fixed charge is the same as or less than that specified sum, and only the balance if it is larger.

If, however, the fixed amount only buys 50 per cent of the heating needs of your property, it will be compared to 50 per cent of the specified sum. There are criteria for working out "how much" heating (or cooking, or lighting, or hot water) is provided.

The Supplementary Benefit Scheme is administered by local offices of the Department of Health and Social Security (DHSS). When you are granted Supplementary Benefit, you should be issued with a form, to go to the local authority, for use in your application for housing benefit. The purpose of this is to avoid dual means-testing.

The form may not be complete. Authorities may need to seek further information from you. If the information the authority require is still not enough, perhaps because you cannot find out what you need to know from the landlord (for instance, as to what part of the rent is for what services, furniture, etc.), the authority will go back to the DHSS for further investigation to be carried out.

Once benefit is assessed, the authority are to notify you how much is due within fourteen days, making clear whether you are left with any residual charges. The notification will impress upon you the need to inform the authority of any relevant changes in circumstances, and of the right to request from the authority a more detailed statement on how the benefit has been assessed (in order to consider the right to call for a review – see below).

It is this notification which should reveal whether you have been treated in some way other than how you believe you ought to have been treated, such as because a non-dependant deduction has been made, or a deduction of the wrong class.

You are under a duty to notify the authority if you cease to qualify for Supplementary Benefit, or if there is a change in the non-dependants or sub-tenants living in the property, or a change in the rent or rates received from a sub-tenant, or in your rent or rates.

There is a similar but much wider duty to inform the DHSS of changes, of which the DHSS will warn someone who is receiving Supplementary Benefit. The two classes of authority – local and DHSS – may be expected to "cross-inform" each other.

If you cease to qualify for Supplementary Benefit, the DHSS will issue a cancellation certificate. This will not be so, however, for Supplementary Benefit recipients who go into hospital, who may lose their Supplementary Benefit but will carry on receiving their housing benefit for an additional eight weeks.

Otherwise, the entitlement to housing benefit will cease, although the authority should immediately and automatically inform the applicant of the right to reapply, i.e. as a standard case (see below).

If a successful standard case application is received within one month of the date of cessation (as a certificated case), your new benefit should be backdated so that there has been no gap.

If you live in a hostel, and receive board, none of this will apply to you. You will not qualify for Housing Benefit at all. Instead, you should receive an amount for both board and lodging in your Supplementary Benefit payment.

B. Standard Cases

The basic principles are to calculate: (a) the eligible rent and rates; (b) your income; and (c) a "needs allowance" for the household as a whole. The needs allowance is deducted from income, and the balance determines how much housing benefit will be paid.

This does not mean that the whole balance is paid. Only a fixed proportion, which is changed from time to time – for example, 60 per cent – of elegible rent and rates will be met by benefit.

If income is above needs allowance, a lower percentage will be paid; where income is below needs allowance, a higher percentage will be paid. The proportions may vary and are more generous if you are or your partner is a pensioner.

Similarly, the needs allowance will depend upon factors such as whether you are or partner is a pensioner, or registered disabled. The needs allowances are specified by the government and consist of various fixed amounts applicable to different households, in different circumstances.

Income taken into account is from all sources, including other welfare benefits, such as Child Benefit and maintenance payments in respect of children.

Where you are earning, authorities will normally base your assessment on the five weeks before application (if paid weekly), or the two months before (if paid monthly).

Authorities may, however, average out earnings over different periods, if the recent period has been exceptional, i.e. exceptionally high (for instance, because of a lot of overtime), or exceptionally low (for instance, because of short hours).

If you are self-employed, business expenses should be deducted; that is to say, your income should be treated as the same as that on which you have to pay tax.

The authority may disregard some classes of income, such as attendances and mobility allowances of the disabled, war disablement or war widow's pension, charitable payments, industrial disablement allowance or pension.

They may disregard a maintenance payment, and travel allowances and other parts of payments to those attending government training schemes. In addition, they should disregard income which will itself be deducted from the elegible rent, i.e. payments by sub-tenants and possibly those by non-dependants.

Normally it is only your income and that of your partner which is to be taken into account. If, however, the authority believes that there would otherwise be an abuse of public funds, it may assess entitlement on the basis of the income of a non-dependant who lives in the household and who has a higher income than you – for example, if a person with a high income transferred a tenancy or licence to a person with a low income (not his or her partner) in order to take advantage of the scheme.

If given benefit, you are under a general duty to inform the authority of any change in your circumstances which you might reasonably expect to affect your entitlement to benefit.

C. Worse-Off Cases

I have already described why it is that you may find yourself in a worse-off position because of the existence of the housing benefit scheme, i.e. because without housing benefit you *would* qualify for

Supplementary Benefit, whereas with housing benefit you do not, *and* the extent to which you benefit accordingly suffers.

This can arise because the basis for calculating needs allowance in standard cases and for calculating basic Supplementary Benefit are not exactly the same.

"Worse-off cases" are treated as standard cases, but with an additional allowance, known as "housing benefit supplement". To qualify for housing benefit supplement, you must have both *claimed* and been *assessed* for Supplementary Benefit,*and* housing benefit. This is the one case where you are dually means-tested.

The supplement is paid to those who would qualify for Supplementary Benefit, but who fail so to qualify because of excessive *income*.

Excessive *income* is not the only reason for failure to qualify for Supplementary Benefit: you can also be disqualified by capital in excess of £3,000, full-time employment, or because you are engaged in a trade dispute. Disqualification for these reasons will not entitle you to housing benefit supplement.

DHSS offices are supposed to keep a stock of local authority, standard-case application forms. If you are disqualified from Supplementary Benefit for excess income, they should provide you with a copy of the local-authority application form, on which they should write the amount of the excess income. Alternatively, they may write separately to the authority. In either event, they should advise you to make an application to the authority.

Once you go to the authority, it will make an assessment in the normal way. It will then be able to identify how much of your housing costs will *not* be met by standard housing benefit. That is to say, it can see what the balance you have to pay will be.

(This is the balance of *eligible* housing costs, and has nothing to do with the question of deductions from rent for sub-tenants, non-dependants, non-qualifying costs and so on). If the balance is more than the Supplementary Benefit excess income amount, you are a worse-off case and qualify for the housing benefit supplement.

An example may help. Say that you qualify for Supplementary Benefit. Housing costs will be met in full. Say you fail to qualify by £15 per week. You go to the local authority and find that standard benefit meets all but £6 of your rent. Even if you were receiving 100 per cent rent (as a certificated case), your income would still be £9 per week above Supplementary Benefit level (£15 less £6). But if standard benefit would leave you with £20 rent to pay for yourself, then you are worse off with housing benefit than without it, by £5 per week.

The full amount of this difference should be met by housing benefit supplement. This will also entitle you to a number of other benefits (not related to housing – for example, free school meals and milk, assistance with prescription charges, and optical or dental charges, Christmas bonus for those on Supplementary Benefit where this applies, special "one-off" Supplementary Benefits, increases for being on benefit for more than twelve months, known as the long-term rate).

In other words, you ought to be put back in the same position as if housing benefit had not knocked you out of Supplementary Benefit.

The system may be expected to work if you go *first* to the DHSS. What about when you go first to the local authority? It is not experienced in assessing for Supplementary Benefit. Nor does it have any obligation to do so. There will be no statement of "excess income" with which to compare the balance of eligible rent which you have to meet.

The scheme does not adequately deal with this. The DHSS has issued some "rule-of-thumb" guidance, to help authorities identify cases which may qualify, who should of course be advised to make an application for Supplementary Benefit, and put the proper machinery in train. Authorities at a local level may by way of co-operation with local offices of the DHSS enter into arrangements to help them spot these cases.

Nevertheless, you should be very careful to remain aware of this possibility, and if in doubt should always make an application to the DHSS, for Supplementary Benefit, either when first considering applying for housing benefit or at any later time. Pensioners, in particular, are quite likely to fall into this class and should always check.

Someone who qualifies for housing benefit supplement is in other respects a "standard case" and it follows that you are under duty to notify the authority of any change in your circumstances which you might reasonably expect to affect your entitlement.

How and when will benefit be paid?

The major difference under this heading is between those who are tenants or licensees of local authorities and development corporations, and those who rent from housing associations.

The former will not receive any cash, because their benefit will be deducted from their rent (and if separate, rates) payments. They are said to receive a ''rebate'' (i.e. they pay rebated amounts).

The latter, however, receive their benefit (save in those circumstances where it is paid direct to the landlord: see below) and pass it on, as part or all of their rent or rates payment. They are said to receive an ''allowance''.

This difference aside, the main principles are the same. Normally, a claim for housing benefit is to be processed by the authority within fourteen days. If the authority has to obtain further information, the fourteen days run from the date when it gets the last information it has asked for, in order to enable us to make its decision.

This will not usually be a problem if you are certificated. If the authority does not have enough information, it notifies the DHSS, whose duty it is to obtain the further information. Only if the DHSS fails to get the information it seeks from you, which could lead it to cancel the certificate, will the failure to provide information cost you benefit.

In other cases, you should always be quick to provide whatever information the authority needs, because a delay may cost you money, in terms of when the benefit starts. If you fail to answer a request from the authority for information necessary to the calculation of housing benefit, for a period of six weeks (without a satisfactory explanation of the delay), the authority may treat the application as wholly withdrawn, and you will have to start over again.

If the authority has not given its determination within fourteen days, and you are a certificated tenant or licensee of a housing association, it has to make an interim payment. The interim payment will be no more than you claim, but may be less.

Adjustments will take place at a later date, when the final decision is reached. Otherwise, the authority does not have to pay (or rebate) until it reaches its decision.

The starting date for benefit is different for different cases. Certificated cases start on the same date as that on which the certificate is issued. Normally, benefit is payable on a weekly basis.

When benefit is cancelled, the cancellation takes place from the date of cancellation.

If you have unsuccessfully applied for Supplementary Benefit and *then* apply to the local authority for housing benefit, *within one month*, you will receive your benefit backdated to the date of the claim for Supplementary Benefit.

Standard (and worse-off) cases otherwise receive benefit backdated to the application. In exceptional circumstances, the authority has a *discretion* to back-date for up to twelve months.

It may do this, for example, if there was no application because of illness; or else because you have run into arrears of rent only because of your ignorance of the availability of benefit, and a backdated payment or rebate will clear or reduce the debt.

In certificated cases, the first payment or rebate should normally be made within fourteen days of the issue of the certificate. Otherwise, payments may be made at the discretion of the authority, and will commonly be monthly or four-weekly payments, normally about halfway through the period to which the payment relates.

The payment may be weekly, if the authority thinks that paying over a longer period is likely to lead to overpayment (i.e. because it expects your circumstances to change) or that it is in your interests to do so (for example, where you are known to have difficulty budgeting).

If you are entitled to £2 or more per week, and pay weekly under your agreement, you may require the authority to pay fortnightly, and it has to agree. At the other extreme, it may pay up to six-monthly, where the amount involved is less than 50p per week.

Authorities can decide *how* to pay. They are not supposed to make payments in a way that is unreasonable for occupiers, such as collection from a difficult or inaccessible office.

The payment is normally to you, but can be to the landlord in the following circumstances: (1) if you agree; or (2) where you are more than thirteen weeks in arrears with your rent; or (3) where the DHSS notifies the authority that, under a Supplementary Benefit arrangements, *arrears* of rent are being deducted from Supplementary Benefit and paid direct to a landlord.

In these circumstances, the authority pays the *current* rent allowance direct (in effect, so as to prevent further arrears accruing).

If an authority has reasonable grounds for suspecting that you are not paying rent or rates regularly, it can withhold payment. It has to give you an opportunity to comment before doing this. The payments withheld may be released later, once the authority is satisfied that they will be used for the purposes of meeting your housing costs.

In certificated cases, your qualification for benefit continues so long as the DHSS does not cancel the certificate.

In standard cases, if you are a pensioner, or in receipt of a long-term disability benefit or pension, the assessment can last for up to twelve months (or, if made in October or November of any year, fourteen months). In other cases, the assessment lasts for up to seven months (or nine months, if in March or April).

Immediately on the cancellation of a certificate, or within two months of the expiry of a period of standard benefit, you ought to be invited to reapply, and if the new application is (a) successful and (b) made no more than one month after the end of the previous period, the benefit will be backdated to ensure that there is no gap.

If there have been any overpayments of housing benefit, authorities may reclaim from standard cases, and ought to do so if the overpayment results from, for example, misrepresentation by you, but ought not to do so where you could not reasonably have been expected to appreciate that you were receiving too much.

In certificated cases, repayment can *only* be claimed where the failure is yours – such as because of misrepresentation or failure to disclose relevant information – *not* where it occurs as a result of an error by an official of the authority or the DHSS.

Can I appeal a refusal or an assessment?

Yes. If you are dissatisfied with a decision, you are entitled to ask the authority to review its decision. Initially, an officer will reconsider; if still dissatisfied, you may ask for a review by a "board", which is made up of local councillors. The notification of decision will inform you of the right to ask for a review, and how to do so; it also permits you to seek further details of how your benefit has been calculated, to enable you to decide whether or not to seek a review.

10: Repairs and Improvements

Repairs

Who is responsible for repairs?

The landlord will *usually* be responsible for repairs. Tenants (whether or not secure) have different rights from licensees (again, whether or not secure): see Chapter 2.

A. Tenants

When is the landlord responsible for repairs?

With two exceptions, under a tenancy the landlord is responsible for all major repairs, *whatever the tenancy agreement says.* The exceptions are: (a) tenancies for seven years or more; and (b) tenancies which began before 24 October 1961 (Housing Act 1961).

A tenancy is a tenancy for seven years or more only if it is a fixed-term tenancy for that length of time; a periodic tenancy which has lasted, or may last, longer, will not be a tenancy for seven years or more, and so the landlord will still be responsible.

In deciding whether or not the tenancy began before 24 October 1981, it is the original tenancy which matters: this may be your own, or that of someone to whose tenancy you have succeeded (see Chapter 3).

In these two cases, repairing responsibility will depend on the terms of the agreement; in the latter case (an "old" but long-lived periodic tenancy) there may even be a "gap" in responsibilities. (In this case, however, (a) if your landlord is not the local authority, the authority will still have powers to compel repairs, and (b) whether or not your landlord is the local authority, you may be able to complain to a magistrate: see below on both these subjects).

What are the repairs for which the landlord is responsible?

For the purpose of the repairing obligation described above, "major repairs" means the structure and exterior of the property, and the installations for heating (both the premises, and water) and gas, electricity and water supplies, including basins, sinks, baths and lavatories.

The landlord has to keep all of these elements of a property in proper repair and working order. The right does not extend to, for instance, your own cooker, refrigerator or other installations.

Where you occupy a flat or room, "structure and exterior" includes the outside walls of the flat or room, the floor, and the floor above the ceiling. In other words, the premises are defined as if they were not part of another building.

The structure and exterior of the building itself are *not* in any other way part of the structure and exterior of the flat or room, so that responsibility for them is (save as stated in the next paragraph), a matter of contract. This may be covered by a service charge (see Chapter 8).

There is, however, an *additional* implied term that a landlord will keep common parts of a building with flats or rooms in it in acceptable condition, and this includes not only, for example, halls, stairs, corridors, front door, but also the roof of the building. This does not apply to a house let out as a whole.

These rights do not extend to internal decoration or minor internal repairs. However, if the state of the interior is damaged – as it will be by, for instance, leaks or damp – because of the landlord's failure to keep the premises in repair, the landlord may have to put the interior back into proper condition.

Similarly, if the interior condition is damaged (for example, wallpaper stripped off) to enable the landlord to carry out the repairs for which it is liable, the condition will have to be reinstated.

The rights do not cover damage done by you, or someone living with you, nor do they cover matters which you ought to keep in repair. You are under a general obligation to "use premises in a tenant-like manner", i.e. to use premises reasonably, and normally, and take reasonable care of them.

Thus, if you go away for a long break you should turn off water, electricity and gas as appropriate, cleaning windows, mending fuses, unblocking the sink, "in short . . . the little jobs about the place which a reasonable tenant would do".

You are not, however, expected to do works to prevent "normal wear and tear", which covers the fact that property will deteriorate over time and with use. When "wear and tear" becomes "disrepair", the matter has become one for the landlord.

When deciding whether or not premises are in disrepair, you have to take into account the age, character and locality of the property. A new property may expect to be, and to be kept, in better condition that an old property.

There does come a point when a house is so old and rundown that it requires virtual renewal to be put back into acceptable condition: at that point, however, it is likely to have become unfit for human habitation (see further below).

There are obvious problems which a landlord must attend to: leaking roofs, pipes, and drains, broken or decayed brickwork, doors and windows broken or ill-fitting, plumbing not working and so on.

The hardest question is whether the landlord is obliged to do anything about damp, which affects many properties, both old and new. I do not here mean *penetrating* damp, which will be caused by a broken roof, defective brickwork, leaking pipes or gutters, bad window-frames, etc., because this is clearly a matter of disrepair, within the landlord's obligations. Rather, we are concerned with *rising* and *condensation* dampness.

In a new property, there either will or ought to be a damp-proof course or membrane; this will prevent *rising* damp (or if it does not, it will be the landlord's responsibility to put right).

However, the construction of much new property means that it may suffer from *condensation.* If the condensation is caused by an *unreasonable* use of the property by you – more than a "reasonable amount" of heating, or an "unreasonable" amount of washing without opening the windows – it is *possible* that the disrepair will be considered to have been caused by you. But most public tenants are reasonable and responsible people, and you should not allow yourself to be fobbed off with a claim that it is your fault, unless you agree you have not been behaving sensibly.

If there is condensation-caused dampness, you should take advice as to whether the remedy for it can be classed as a case of disrepair under the obligations already described, or whether it would be better treated as a "statutory nuisance", which is a separate provision, described below.

If you live in an old house, you are less likely to suffer from condensation (but if you do the same points apply), but may well suffer from *rising* damp, because there may not be a damp-proof course or membrane in the property at all.

Whether or not the landlord has to do anything to prevent rising damp where there is no course or membrane will depend both on extent and on cost.

One can ask: is the landlord being asked to turn an old house into a newly modernised one (not within an obligation to repair), or is the job small enough to be classed as a repair? If the rising damp *cannot* be brought within the repairing obligation, it may still be a "statutory nuisance" about which you can complain to a magistrate (see below).

In addition to these repairing obligations, landlords are not allowed to use neighbouring property in their own control in such a way as to damage the property they have let to you; nor, indeed, can any other neighbour.

If works have been carried out to your premises, before or since you moved in, negligently, or in a less than workmanlike manner, any later defects are the responsibility of the landlord and/or the person carrying out the work.

Whose responsibility is it to find out about disrepair?

Yours, for the most part. If your premises are in disrepair, the landlord is not under an obligation to carry out the repairs until it has had notice of it. However, the notice need not come from you: it may be because a neighbour has complained (because of damage being done to his or her property), or because the local authority (if it is not the landlord) has told your landlord (see further below).

It is enough to tell an employee or agent of the landlord. Furthermore, if a representative of the landlord is at the premises, perhaps for another reason or to attend to a different job, and it can later be shown that he or she had noticed disrepair (or, perhaps, a consequence of disrepair, such as serious and obvious damp stains from leaks, etc.), this will be enough "notice".

If you are concerned about disrepair in your home, you will do well to notify the landlord, in writing (keeping a copy of your letter). There can then be no argument about whether or not the landlord was "on notice". You should set out what is wrong as precisely as you can, although if you cannot say what the *cause* is, you can simply describe the *effect*, i.e. "The window won't open." "The lavatory won't flush." "The rain comes in," and so on.

In some cases, the landlord may be considered responsible for remedying disrepair even if you cannot show that notice has been given. This will be true of disrepair in the common parts, in neighbouring property in its own control, and of disrepair caused by defective work it has had carried out.

It may also be true if a court takes the view that the landlord *ought* to have known of the defect in your own premises, and ought to have done something about it.

Obviously, though, the first step is still to ask the landlord to carry out the repairs needed.

Can the landlord enter the premises to inspect for disrepair, or to carry out repairs?

Yes. You have to let the landlord in to *inspect* the state of the premises, provided the landlord calls at a reasonable time of the day, and has given you at least twenty-four hours' notice in writing.

If you do not, you may have broken your tenancy or licence, and this may give rise to a ground for possession (see Chapter 7), although this is only likely to be used to get an order from the court to compel you to admit the landlord (but if you keep doing it, *could* lead to an outright eviction order: see Chapter 7).

As for entry in order to *carry out* repairs, the landlord has the implied right to this, at reasonable times, and on reasonable notice. What is reasonable will depend on all of the circumstances; for example, in an emergency, immediate access will be permissible.

If my landlord wants to repair, should I let it do so?

Generally, yes. You will not, for example, be able to claim compensation (see further below) or otherwise complain about lack of repair if the reason the landlord has been unable to do works is because you would not let it in to do so! Indeed, if you refuse, the landlord may well be able to get an order to force you to let the works be carried out, though if you do not have much security of tenure, the landlord's most likely response will be to bring your right of occupation to an end!

If you have enough security of tenure to be able to enforce your rights (for example, because you are a secure tenant, or because you have some years to run on a fixed-term lease), you should try and ensure that exactly what is to be done, and how long it will take, is put in writing, and signed by both of you. Thus, for example, if the landlord says that works will take three weeks, and will interfere with your use of the bathroom, but they then take ten weeks and interfere with your use of more of the house, you will have grounds for complaint, and damages (compensation), for the difference.

You should also seek compensation, probably by way of reduction in rent, for the period of disruption (having regard to both the length of time your home will be disrupted, and how much of it), as well, of course, as any damages to which you are entitled because of the disrepair *prior* to the works being carried out.

If your landlord wants to do works, you will do best to take advice as to all of these matters, and possibly have an adviser (see Chapter 12) deal with the landlord on your behalf.

If my landlord asks me to move out for works to be done, should I agree?

You do not *have* to move out to let your landlord do works, *unless* the works can only reasonably be carried out with you out of occupation. In this case, as well as having the arrangement in writing, and covering your compensation, as in the last answer, you will need to make sure that there is agreement as to where you will stay while the works are being done, who will pay for alternative temporary accommodation, and who will pay for such other matters as storage of your belongings, electricity, etc., used by repair workers, and so on. Again, you should if possible have all these matters handled by an adviser (see Chapter 12).

If the landlord will not repair, is there anything I can do to make it?

Yes. One course of action is for you to take legal proceedings against it, to get an order to make it carry out the works that are necessary.

If your landlord is not the local authority, another course of action is to complain to the local authority, which has a range of powers with which to force landlords to do works (see further below). In addition, in two cases there is a right of direct complaint to a magistrate.

When can I take legal proceedings myself?

When any of the repairing obligations described above have been broken by the landlord, you will be entitled to use the *civil* courts (see Chapter 12), to obtain an order to carry out the works, *and* for monetary compensation for any loss you have suffered as a result of the landlord's failure.

This may be compensation for direct loss – such as damaged property or clothing, or for less direct loss such as additional heating costs, or eating out because facilities are not working, or even staying elsewhere because the premises became uninhabitable – or it may be for less easily quantifiable loss, such as for ill-health or reduced enjoyment of the premises.

However, you must bear in mind that in most cases the landlord's duty to repair will not start until it has been put on notice (see page 134), and, until the duty to repair has commenced, there will be no breach of duty – in which case, the landlord will not be responsible for loss caused.

It will still have to carry out the repairs, because you will invariably have given forewarning before starting court proceedings, and notice will accordingly, necessarily, have been given.

This limitation on landlord's liability will not apply where the damage is in the common parts, or in neighbouring premises under his or her control, or results from negligent or defective work to your premises, or where a court takes the view that the landlord ought to have known about and repaired the defect (see page 135).

Can I withhold rent to make the landlord do the repairs?

The government now has power to make a "scheme" to let you do this *if – but only if –* you are a *secure* tenant.

At the present time, the scheme for secure tenants to carry out their own repairs has not become law. However, the government have published the *proposals*, and it is likely that the final scheme will be similar to these proposals. The details contained in the proposals are considerable, and the tenant wishing to exercise the right to repair would certainly be well advised to take legal advice first. The description which follows is of the *proposals* only: i.e. they are not yet law.

The right to carry out a repair means the right to carry out a repair for which the *landlord* is responsible under the tenancy (see page 131). There is an exception: the tenant of a flat cannot carry out works to its structure and exterior. You will have to state in a notice claiming the right to repair exactly what obligation the landlord is responsible for, and how it is in breach of it.

The right to repair will apply only to works of a value between £20 and £200 (calculated according to what the landlord would spend on the works, including the landlord's administrative expenses.)

In the notice claiming the right to repair, you will also have to state what works you intend to carry out and with what materials, and whether you intend to carry them out yourself, or hire someone to do so (in which latter case, you will have to identify them). In this latter case, you also have to say whether you are agreeable to direct payment by landlord to your contractor. The landlord has a right of objection on any of these aspects, except where you wish to carry out the works yourselves, so it can object to contractor, works, or materials.

Furthermore, for the period between when you successfully establish your right to repair and when you make your subsequent claim for payment under it, the landlord's obligations to repair which are relevant to the repair you are proposing to carry out yourself are "suspended". This has two results for you. First of all, if any harm comes to you or someone else during this period, it may be impossible to claim against the landlord. Secondly, if you do works badly and later harm is caused to someone else because of it, you will be liable for the consequences!

All the stages in the right to repair have to be carried through by special forms of notice drawn up by the government, and these will tell you more precisely what you have to do. It will, of course, be tempting to go ahead with works, because public landlords can be so slow carrying out repairs. It will be understandable if you decide instead to rely on the fact that you know there is a right to repair. There is, however, relatively little room for you to make money out of it, by doing works for yourself, and a very high risk that you will find that you cannot reclaim the cost at all. Above all, the cost limits mean that the right will not apply to the *major* defects causing you discomfort, such as those which cause damp.

In addition to this scheme (when it becomes law) and operating separately from it (so that none of its rules will apply, such as use of special forms, £20-£200 limit), *all* tenants have a *theoretical* right to use the rent "against" disrepair. However, in practice, this is an extremely dangerous tactic, because if, at the end of the day, for this reason or that (want of notice, not landlord's responsibility, not bad enough disrepair, etc.), you are shown to be wrong, you will be in rent arrears.

While this should not cause an outright order for possession against a secure tenant, it may do so against a non-secure tenant (see Chapter 7), and in any event it will worsen your position.

The right is to withhold rent in order to pay for works of repair which are the landlord's responsibility, and even to compensate yourself for losses you can claim from the landlord.

Most major repairs, however, will cost far more than you will be able to pay out of the rent, however long it is accumulated, and there is an obvious risk that you will be more generous compensating yourself for losses than a court will be.

Where you do decide to run the risk of withholding rent and having works carried out yourself, perhaps if they are relatively minor, you should always give the landlord (a) an opportunity to do the work itself, (b) a warning of your intentions, (c) a copy of estimates (and you should obtain at least two estimates, preferably three), and (d) the choice of reimbursing you directly or having the money stopped from the rent. Each such warning or notification to the landlord should be in writing, you should always keep a copy of the letter and you should at each stage permit the landlord a reasonable opportunity to reply, or put the works in hand.

When can the local authority force my landlord to repair?

If your landlord is not the local authority itself, the authorities have a range of powers which they can use. Some of these proceedings involve criminal prosecutions of the landlord, others do not.

The authority may take proceedings against a landlord where there is what is known as a "statutory nuisance". This means *either* that the premises are in such a state that there is a risk to your health or that of any other occupant, *or* that there is a defect in common parts or neighbouring premises under the landlord's control, which is causing harm in your premises.

The local authority also has powers in relation to: insufficient numbers of lavatories, or lavatories in an unsatisfactory state; insufficient food-storage space; and, vermin. (Although the powers are wide enough to make *you* rather than the landlord cure this defect, they will almost certainly only do this if the presence of vermin is your fault.)

The authority also has powers related to unfitness for human habitation, serious disrepair (designed to prevent premises becoming unfit for human habitation), and conditions such as might interfere with your personal comfort (such as dangerous wiring, or dampness not enough to be prejudicial to your health or to qualify the premises as unfit for human habitation).

These powers are cumulative, that is to say that they can all be used if necessary, and although an authority will normally select and use one only first, if that fails, they may try another power.

However, as we are dealing with public landlords, it must be said that the local authority will only use any of these powers as a last resort, and will first try – and allow what you may well consider far too much time for – a "negotiated solution" (i.e. works by agreement).

The unfitness provisions are the principal powers used by authorities, not least because if they find that premises *are* unfit for human habitation, they eventually *have* to take action. The action they may take depends on whether the premises can be made fit at a reasonable expense or not. If they can, the authority serves a repairs notice; if they cannot, the authority take action which will normally lead to an agreement or an order not to use the premises for human habitation any longer.

Such an order will mean that it is illegal for you to go on living in the premises. However, in these cases, the authority also has to rehouse you (see Chapter 1). You will not be prosecuted unless you have been offered, and have refused, a reasonable alternative property.

In addition, when such an order is made, you will normally be entitled to compensation for having to move. How much compensation will depend on the amount of time you have been in occupation – you should get a minimum of the reasonable costs of moving, but may get a cash payment as well. The payments are known as "home loss payment", and "disturbance payment".

Unfitness means that the premises are *so* defective in relation to one or more of the following matters that they are not reasonably suitable for occupation in that condition: repairs; stability; freedom from damp; internal arrangement (for example, steep or insecure stairs, bathroom or toilet leading off from kitchen or living-room, sudden changes in floor level); natural lighting; ventilation; water supply; drainage and sanitary conveniences; and facilities for preparing and cooking food and for disposing of waste water.

It follows that a major defect in one respect could lead to a finding of unfitness, or that several minor defects could do so. In one case, the only window in one of the bedrooms of a small house had a broken sashcord and could only be opened at risk of injury. This meant that the house could not properly be ventilated.

"If the state of repair of a house is such that by ordinary user [use] damage may naturally be caused to the occupier, either in respect of personal injury to life or limb, or injury to health, then the house is not in all respects fit for human habitation."

This does not mean, of course, that *every* broken sashcord will make *every* house unfit for human habitation, simply that something as small and apparently as trivial or as easy to repair *may* have that effect.

Can I force the authority to take action?

You can only force the local authority to take action against your landlord if the authority is under a *duty* to do so, as distinct from when it merely has *power* to do so. Even when there is a duty, it is extremely difficult to force authorities to take action, because so often it is a mere matter of *opinion* whether or not their duty has arisen – for example, whether or not there is a statutory nuisance, or premises are actually unfit.

In either case, though (duty or power), you can complain to the Local Ombudsman (see Chapter 11) about the inaction of your authority. This should be done by asking your local councillor to forward your complaint, but if he or she will not do so, you can still ask the Local Ombudsman to look into the matter. The Local Ombudsman cannot order the authority to do anything, but can make a finding of maladministration, i.e. that the authority has not behaved as properly as it ought. Such a finding usually results in corrective action by the authority.

When can I complain to a magistrate?

You can go direct to a magistrate about unfitness, or about statutory nuisance.

If you complain about unfitness, and the magistrate agrees that your home is unfit for human habitation, he or she will direct the matter to the local authority's attention. Although you may already have been to the authority, without success, it will prompt it (though not require it) to look further into the matter, and report back to the magistrate, if only as a matter of courtesy to him or her.

This procedure will not amount to a prosecution of your landlord. It is, however, an especially useful procedure if your landlord is the local authority itself. This is because a local authority cannot take action against itself, so that, even if it *ought* to apply the same standards to itself as it could and would apply to another, it cannot be *forced* to do so.

Using this complaint procedure goes at least some of the distance towards getting an official agreement (that of the magistrate) that your premises are unfit, and drawing attention to the problem. Even more effective, however, is prosecution for statutory nuisance, which *can* lead to the criminal conviction of the authority. This may be used when the conditions for statutory nuisance are fulfilled (see page 139).

It is particularly useful where condensation is involved, which might not amount to a breach of the tenancy obligation to repair (see above). The same is true of rising damp in an older property.

In connection with condensation, there is clear legal authority for the proposition that if the premises are vulnerable to condensation (for instance, open to the elements, inadequate heating, a particular type of construction which leaves the structure of the building "cold", so that condensation forms when normal "heat" – including body heat – is to be found inside), the landlord will be guilty of statutory nuisance if it does nothing about it.

You should always have given notice to the landlord that, if it does not cure the defect, you will take such proceedings, and when you start the proceedings, you should specify exactly what is wrong and, if possible, how it should be cured. You will need assistance to bring these proceedings (see Chapter 12).

B. Licensees

When is the landlord responsible for the repairs?

If you are a licensee, whether or not a secure licensee (see Chapter 2), the landlord will probably be liable for *all* repairs.

The agreement may say otherwise. This may be because, for example, the licence is of short-life property scheduled for redevelopment, and it is at the heart of the arrangement that you have been allowed in for a short time, in the present state of the premises, in effect *because* they are in such bad condition.

If, however, you have a licence because you live in a hostel, or, for example, because you have tied accommodation, it will be the landlord's responsibility to keep the premises in a condition fit for the purpose for which they were let. As a rule of thumb this will be taken to mean in an internal condition approximating to that in which they appeared to be when let, and externally and structurally in a condition good enough to keep the premises in the same sort of state, i.e. wind and weathertight.

What about notice?

This is not formally required before you can complain of breach of your agreement, because if you are a licensee, the landlord has much greater control over the premises than if you are a tenant. However, it never hurts to give notice, and always improves your own position.

Can I get a court order to force the landlord to repair?

Yes; if the landlord is in breach of your agreement, then you can always get a court to order the landlord to comply. However, if you are a non-secure licensee, you will have to bear your limited security in mind.

You will also be entitled to compensation for damage to your own property through damp, etc., or for having to stay elsewhere because, for example, your room was uninhabitable.

However, again, all your rights are much less because you are a licensee: you would not get the cost of alternative accommodation for long, maybe for only a few days, because, as a licensee, you would not have lost the same extent of rights as a tenant. (This would be less true of a *secure* licensee, whose position is probably the same as a tenant: there are, however, few of these.)

If my landlord is not the local authority, can the local authority use powers to force the landlord to repair?

Yes. Most of the powers of the local authority described above apply just as much to licensees as to tenants. However, if you are evicted as a result – because, for example, a closing order is placed on the premises, or an undertaking given to the authority that the premises will no longer be used for human habitation – while you will still get rehousing (*unless* you are a short-life occupier), you are much less likely to get compensation (see above).

Can I complain to a magistrate?

Yes. Your rights are exactly the same as those of tenants (see above).

Improvements

Do I have the right to carry out improvements to my home?

Secure tenants (Chapter 2) have a "right to improve" their own dwellings. Other occupiers only have such a right if the agreement says so.

For the purpose of the "right to improve", an improvement includes addition or alteration to a dwelling, putting up an external television or radio aerial and external decorations.

The written consent of the landlord must be obtained, but the landlord cannot refuse consent unreasonably, i.e. for no reason at all, whimsically, or out of stubbornness. If a landlord refuses consent, it must give a statement of reasons, also in writing. You may challenge your landlord's refusal of consent, by issuing proceedings in a county court for a declaration by a judge that the refusal was unreasonable and that you may therefore go ahead.

Among the reasons which will be considered acceptable are that the "improvement" would make the dwelling less safe, or would make neighbouring premises less safe, or because it would mean the landlord has to incur extra expenditure (for example, on works to an estate which will be more difficult and costly because of the alteration), or because the improvement would mean that if you quit, the landlord will get less rent for the premises, or a lower price on a sale.

You should think very carefully before deciding to improve, whether under the agreement or under the statutory right. While your rent will probably not increase on account of the works you carry out (see below), your rates may do so, and in any event you will be spending money on property that is not ultimately your own and that you may not be able to stay in for ever (such as where you fall on hard times and suffer eviction for arrears).

If I improve, can the landlord raise the rent?

No. Provided you had the right to carry out the works in question, and either paid for the works, or but for an improvement grant (see below) would have paid for the works, the rent under a secure tenancy cannot be increased on account of the improvements so long as you remain the tenant, or, if you die, your spouse remains the tenant.

Similarly, if you have succeeded to a spouse's tenancy (see Chapter 3), the rent under a secure tenancy cannot be increased on account of such improvements carried out by your deceased spouse. However, if children or other members of the family succeed to the secure tenancy, or it is transferred while the tenant is still alive, or if there is an exchange of secure tenancy (see Chapter 3), rents *can* be increased on account of the improvements by the person taken over from.

Will improvements increase the price on right to buy?

Not normally (see Chapter 5).

Can I get an improvement grant?

An improvement grant *may* be available from the local authority (whether or not it is also your landlord). Be warned, though, that improvement grants are deceptive entities.

You cannot get an improvement grant to do whatever you want: if you apply, the local authority decides what *must* be done in order to qualify for grant-aid *at all*. This produces a schedule of works, and a resulting cost. The improvement grant, however, will not be for this full cost, but to a government-specified limit, which is often much lower than the cost of the schedule specified by the authority. Even then, it is still not the amount specified by the government which is paid, but an "appropriate percentage" of that amount, which may be as little as 50 per cent, and only occasionally rises to 90 per cent, and even less frequently to the full 100 per cent.

Can my landlord be forced to carry out improvements?

No. The powers to compel improvement which apply in the private sector do not apply to public landlords.

Can my landlord carry out improvements voluntarily?

If you consent – yes. If the improvement means that the premises, after works, will not be suitable for you any longer – for example, because there will be a room less, or for other reasons – then you will have to move. You will, however, be entitled to disturbance payment, and perhaps also home-loss payment, in the same way as on a closing order (see above). This applies even if your landlord is the local authority.

Be careful of "options". These arise when it is possible for you to move back but the landlord persuades you to "opt" for permanent removal elsewhere. If you *could* in practice move back, and choose to move elsewhere permanently, you may any right to compensation.

If you do not wish to let the landlord carry out the improvements, then whether or not it has a right to do so depends on your security.

If you are a *periodic* secure tenant or licensee, they will have to get a court order, and works of improvement is one of the grounds for possession (see Chapter 7).

If you have a *fixed-term* secure tenancy, or licence (though this is unlikely), then unless the agreement specifically provides for the landlord to carry out improvements (also unlikely) there will be nothing the landlord can do until the end of the fixed period, and even then it will still need a court order (see Chapter 7).

If you have a periodic non-secure right of occupation, the short answer is that if the landlord wants to improve, it can terminate your agreement and evict you. You will do better to co-operate, in the hope of alternative housing.

If you have a fixed-term non-secure agreement, then again, unless the agreement permits the landlord to carry out improvements, the landlord will not be able to require you to permit the improvements, unless and until the arrangement comes to an end. It may be in your interest to agree, however, if this will affect the grant of a new term, which you want.

11: Collective and Political Action

Why a chapter on collective and political action?

At the beginning of the book (Chapter 1) I drew attention to specific features of the public sector (in contrast to the private sector) when answering the question "Do I want to become a public tenant?"

I described public landlordism as "unmotivated by profit". I also said that "there are pressures which may be put on the landlord, not confined to the individual legal remedies . . . but by way of concerted, political action.. . .

"Throughout [public sector tenants] are dealing with landlords who are in some sense 'publicly accountable', either directly, because the landlord is an elected local authority, or indirectly, because none of the public landlords can afford to attract continuing adverse publicity from the media.

"The very purpose of public landlords is to serve their tenants, and this is undermined when tenant-dissatisfaction mounts to a point when the public itself starts to pay attention to it . . . when problems arise . . . there are more 'weapons' available to the public tenant. . . .'

It is to these remarks that I wish to address attention in this chapter. I wish to do so from two points of view. First of all, the point of view adopted throughout this book has been to describe the *individual* rights of the *individual* tenant (hence, *The Public Tenant's Handbook* – i.e. the apostrophe is deliberately before the "s").

The "right" (or privilege) to "use" this additional "weapon" of collective or political action may be viewed as one more *individual* right, one more way of getting what you want in relation to your home.

If what you want is an aspiration shared or approved by others in your locality, you may enjoy the benefit of group (collective) action, and so long as what you want is apparently reasonable, even if there are not, or you cannot find, other tenants to help put pressure on the landlord, you will be able to enjoy the benefit of media (political) "action" (i.e. publicity).

The second point of view follows logically on from the first.

That is, the point of view of a group of tenants, viewed as such.

There is not a lot which can or ought to be said by way of advice to tenants' associations or other organisations, because every locality is different, the circumstances – including the aspirations of the group – are always different, and, ultimately, no one knows better what ought to be done about housing than those who live in it.

What *is* a tenants' association?

The name "tenants' association" is given to any group of tenants who wish to call themselves that. It means what it says: an association, and it is not necessary that it should be formed into a "legal association" or "society" or "company".

Sometimes, an association of people living locally will include owner-occupiers, in which case the association may be called a residents' association, or residents' and tenants' association, etc. The association may, as another example, be limited to the tenants of one landlord, such as of a housing association or of a local authority, in which case it may be more particularly described.

It matters not what the association is called, as long as it makes the fundamental point: tenants are banding together to fight for their rights *as tenants*, as collectively as in a union or other "work-based" association. People acting together are vastly stronger than people acting alone.

Traditionally, tenants have been "separated". This is still true of the private sector (although there have been times in the past when private-sector tenants have banded together, and recently tenants of particular private landlords have formed associations to fight shoulder-to-shoulder for improved conditions). It has been their separation which has contributed to their vulnerability. Vulnerability comes from other sources, too. Lack of security – loss of home – is a natural fear. It is all very well making a lot of noise about rent-strikes or other action, but what if, one day, it is to be *you* and *your* family who are, quite literally, on the streets?

In the past, vulnerability has also come from an utterly wrong-headed idea, postulated and propagated through the media, predominantly upper- and middle-class owned and operated, that public tenants are the recipients of "charity" (i.e. subsidy), and ought to be – if I may so put it – "bloody grateful they've got anywhere to live". I call this utterly wrong, because, after all, no one asked to be born, and the right to shelter – housing – ought, accordingly, to be an absolute right, or entitlement, following *from the mere fact of being alive.*

(I do not doubt that reasonable arguments exist about "social contract", fundamental rights qualified by duties, such as to work for a living, and prove that you are working by paying for your housing; it is, rather, a question of which comes first – basic right, or social obligation? Furthermore, at a time of massive unemployment, the "social contract/duty" argument wears a little thin! Even when there is enough employment, to make the right to shelter dependent on earning an income means, in effect, that you are tied to your job more than by what the employer has "bought", i.e. your labour.)

Another media-supported myth is that public tenants don't behave properly, and cannot be trusted with decent quality housing. "Coals in the bath", they used to say. (The modern equivalent is "intentional pregnancy", i.e. the spectre of people becoming pregnant in order to qualify for public housing – see Chapter 1 – or "lie back and think of the local authority!")

These myths undermine action by individual tenants: you know that things like that are said and that people believe them – or, the media so take them for granted that it seems they have become virtual "facts".

Adding myth to traditional insecurity to the "charity" school of thought, means that the public tenant has been – at least to some extent – effectively put in a position where it is easier to keep quiet and suffer, than to attract a vast amount of adverse and possibly public attention to yourself. This has been coupled to two propositions of "law". First of all, the law has until recently largely left public tenants' rights in the discretion of their landlords. Rights which are discretionary are not really rights at all: they only become rights when they can be *enforced.*

Secondly, lawyers have not exactly won a hard-earned reputation for helping the poor fight for greater freedoms or conditions. There have been some, but few. Rather, lawyers are those seen peering over the shoulder of the landlord, or standing out in front waving a summons for possession (eviction).

They are expensive, too. Legal aid – described in the next chapter – is a relatively recent entitlement. Before legal aid, those who could not afford lawyers either went without, or had to make shift with "part-time, voluntary, charitable" legal assistance. We are back close to where we started: not rights, but a handout.

This is mostly "old history". It is also the position in which the *individual* tenant either *has been,* or has *felt* himself or herself to have been. (It makes little difference.) The attitude of many landlords has actively encouraged this self-perception, because it keeps the heat off them. It is old history, in the main, because the law now contains a large number of positive, enforceable rights (described in the book up to now, and Chapter 12 for legal aid). But though old history, we cannot ignore it: it is the background, and ideas of the sort I have been describing have a tendency to linger on long after they are dead.

It has not, however, been the history of tenants' associations. It has *coloured* the history of tenants' associations, because, inevitably, the starting-point has always been what tenants already have (and the end, what they are aiming at).

Tenants' associations have – or tenant collective action has – been responsible for forcing through many changes (such as the Rent Acts, so vital in the private sector). Once tenants have banded together, too, they form a powerful group of *voters*. Displease them, and local or indeed general elections can be lost; please them, and it can even make an impact on who runs the country – consider the right to buy, and the 1979 election.

It is at this point that we can turn around and look at the position of the public landlord. It exists to provide housing: what a condemnation when its "clients" (you, the tenants) reject its service as inadequate!

It operates with public subsidy; a loud enough cry from the tenants can result in investigation which shows that public funds have simply been wasted, on housing no better than torn tents.

Even the housing associations have to get public funds, and until recently did so from local authorities (although now they get most of their money from central government, through the Housing

Corporation: see Chapters 2 and 12). Why should money continue to be pumped in to an association whose tenants are up in arms?

Tenants' associations can and do provide support – solidarity – for the individual tenant who remains ambivalent about taking on a fight alone. They can and do attract media attention; they add up to a power, at least local, potentially national; no one can safely ignore them.

How do I find if there is a tenants' association in area?

Ask around. If other tenants cannot tell you, one of the advice or aid organisations described in Chapter 12 will know.

Can I form a tenants' association, if there isn't one in my area?

Yes. It needs relatively few people, with enthusiasm and a little time, and who agree what it is they are dissatisfied with, and/or what it is they want. Again, aid or advice agencies may be able to provide guidance, resources (typing, copying facilities, a place to meet, etc.), or put you in touch with other organisations.

You do not need to be a community worker, or to have the use of one, in order to form a tenants' association, although if the area is not enthusiastic, or if, having started a tenants' association, you find it difficult to keep going, a community worker may be of value for a period, above all to bring you the experiences of others, in similar situations.

The main places where you will get support, guidance and assistance, however, and to whom you should write if thinking along these lines are: The National Tenants' Organisation, the address of your local branch of which may be found out from your landlord, a CAB, or the London Tenants' Organisation, 17 Victoria Park Square, London E2 (tel: 01- 981 1221).

You may also find that your landlord is by no means opposed to an association, and may itself provide funds or other resources with which it can be formed and function.

Will public landlords co-operate with tenants' associations?

With one exception, they do not have to consult with or even communicate with tenants' associations, as a matter of law; in practice, none of the public landlords we are concerned with in this book can afford to ignore them altogether. If for no other reason, it would look very bad indeed in the public eye if media attention is later brought to bear.

If the landlord has provided funding or other support for an association, it is extremely likely to co-operate with it.

The one legal exception relates to service charges, which are not of much importance in the public sector (see Chapter 8). They are accordingly described in greater detail in *The Private Tenant's Handbook*. The provisions for monitoring service charges include formal recognition of, and communication with, tenants' associations.

Will a tenants' association be able to affect housing policies or tenancy agreements?

Leaving aside particular issues which crop up in different areas (such as an unsafe tower block or a bad estate), there is one time when a tenants' association will always be of value.

Since 1980, public landlords have been under a duty to make, and maintain, "consultation arrangements". (Development Corporations – see Chapter 2 – can obtain exemption from these provisions, from the Secretary of State for the Environment). The arrangements are to be those which *the landlord* considers appropriate to enable secure tenants who are likely to be affected by matters of "housing management" to know what the landlord is proposing, and to make their views known to the landlord before any change takes place.

Matters of "housing management" are those which *the landlord* thinks: (a) relate to management, maintenance, improvement or demolition of its housing let to secure tenancies, or the provision of services or facilities to or in connection with such housing, *and* (b) represent a new programme of such works, or a change in practice or policy, *and* (c) are likely to substantially affect all of its secure tenants, or a group of them. For this purpose, a "group" means a social group, or tenants of a particular type of housing, or tenants of an area (such as a local authority ward).

Rent and other charges (Chapter 8) are, however, wholly exempt from these provisions.

Before making any decision on a matter of housing management, the landlord has to invoke the "consultation machinery" it has devised, and take tenants' representations into account.

These provisions will sometimes be in addition to those considered in Chapter 6 (if a change is proposed for all or a whole group of secure tenants), but sometimes Chapter 6 methods of variation will be all that is necessary, because the change does *not* affect all or a group.

If there is a tenants' association in your area, it may well be recognised by the landlord as "part" of its "consultation machinery", i.e. it may make specific provision for notifying associations and for receiving the representations of associations. (This is a circumstance when a public landlord may provide funds for a tenants' association).

Even if there is no formal recognition by the landlord in question, representations made by an association will carry much more weight – and will be capable of being represented in the media much more clearly – than those of individual tenants.

(When individual tenants make individual representations, a lot depends on *how* they are *interpreted*, i.e. by landlord's officers. The officers may classify representations in different ways, or not at all, so as to be able to say, for example, that there is no great opposition to a proposal. A tenants' association will co-ordinate the answers to the questions, and prevent this sort of "breakdown" of replies.)

Can the landlord's opinion as to what is a matter it has to consult on, or as to what is appropriate consultation machinery, be challenged?

On the face of it, when Parliament leaves a matter to a local authority or other landlord, their performance will not be challenged in or by the courts.

However, where public *authorities* – which here means local authorities and development corporations – are involved, the law *will* intervene if it can be shown that they are performing their duties in such a way that *no* reasonable authority could possibly carry them out in that way.

They will also intervene if the authority has failed to take something into account which it ought to have taken into account, or if it has taken something irrelevant into account, or if it has behaved grossly unfairly, or in bad faith, etc.

You will need advice and assistance (see Chapter 12), not merely to launch a challenge, but to identify whether what the authority has done, or failed to do, qualifies for challenge *in law,* not just because *in your opinion* it has behaved badly.

Can landlords be challenged for not following their own consultation procedures?

A public authority (see last answer) certainly can; a housing association landlord probably can as well. Seek advice and assistance (see Chapter 12).

How can I find out what the consultation procedures are?

Local authority and development corporation (if not exempt) landlords have to publish details of their consultation arrangements, and make them available for inspection at their principal office by any member of the public. They must also provide a copy, on payment of "a reasonable fee", to any member of the public who asks for one.

Landlords that are housing associations have a similar duty to publish their arrangements, and to provide a copy on demand for payment of a reasonable fee. However, instead of keeping it at their principal office, they must send a copy to the Housing Corporation, and to the district council or London Borough Council of any area in which they have secure tenancies, and it is then that council's duty to keep the arrangements available for inspection.

12: Legal Proceedings, Advice and Assistance

Where will legal proceedings take place?

Legal proceedings can take place in a number of places. Legal proceedings, strictly so-called, are always in a court. This may be a civil court or a criminal court.

The civil court will usually be the county court, but may be the High Court. It will be the High Court if included in your case against your landlord is a claim for compensation for more than £5,000 (for example, for disrepair). It will also be the High Court if what you are trying to do is to challenge the way a public *authority* (local, or development corporation) has carried out (or failed to carry out) its duties (see, for example, Chapters 1, 7, 8, 10 and 11).

A criminal case will always *start* in the magistrate's court but may go to the Crown Court for the full trial. In addition, proceedings may be heard in a Rent Tribunal (for the rent or security of a retricted contract – see Chapter 2) or Rent Officer or Rent Assessment Committee (for rent under a housing association tenancy – see Chapter 8).

Will legal proceedings always take a long time?

The law is notorious for its delays. Usually, it will take a long time to reach the *end* of a trial, and, therefore, a *final* judgment or order. However, in cases of extreme urgency, such as serious disrepair, homelessness, it is *possible* to get an ''interim'' order from a court with some immediacy. You will need advice and assistance (see below) on this. This only applies in the civil courts, not the criminal courts.

Can I get legal aid?

You can get proper legal aid to bring or defend a civil case, but only to defend a criminal case. It is for this reason that I have given few details in this book about your right to prosecute your landlord for some of the offences it may commit in relation to your tenancy. To give you enough advice to enable you to prosecute on your own would require very much more space than this book allows – almost a book of its own.

That means you would have to use the services of a lawyer to prosecute. (This is not so in the case of a complaint of unfitness to a magistrate, but probably is so even in the case of a complaint of a statutory nuisance: see Chapter 10. In the latter case, however, there are several advice and aid agencies with enough experience to help you prosecute: they will not charge for their services – see further below.)

In a civil case, before a court, legal aid is means-tested. Means-testing is carried out on behalf of the legal-aid authorities by the Department of Health and Social Security. This will mean an appointment additional to those you will have to keep with your lawyer: always try to keep this appointment or you may lose your right to legal aid.

Some lawyers are not keen on legal-aid work (while others do little else). You would do well to consult an advice or aid agency about which lawyers you can expect to give you a friendly reception if you are proceeding under legal aid. This is useful for another reason: because traditionally not many lawyers have specialised in legal-aid work, some are not very experienced at it. Checking with an advice or aid agency increases your chances of finding a competent lawyer.

Legal aid exists to cover your legal costs, including such related costs as those of a surveyor in a repairs case.

You may qualify for legal aid with a "nil contribution", i.e. the whole of your legal costs will be met; or you may not qualify because of your income; or, you may qualify subject to a contribution towards your costs.

If you are on a nil contribution and you lose your case, you will normally not have to pay anything to the other side. If you have to pay a contribution to your own costs, and lose, you may have to pay an equal amount to the other side.

If you win, the other side should pay your costs, but be warned that this may be on a lower rate than your own lawyer is entitled to charge, so there could end up a balance to be met out of legal aid (and, in turn, that may mean that part of your contribution is still payable). If you win on legal-aid, and the landlord has to pay you any compensation, the legal aid authorities are entitled to recoup out of that sum any money they have had to pay, for example because you are on a nil contribution, and the landlord's payment of your costs is not payment in full.

There is no full legal aid for proceedings before a Rent Officer, Tribunal or Assessment Committee.

Can I conduct a case myself?

I have already remarked that to conduct a criminal case yourself would be so difficult that, with no legal aid available, I have hardly bothered to refer to the possibility at all. It is also true that it is difficult to conduct your own case in the civil courts, and if legal aid is available it would be preferable to use the services of a lawyer.

You do not have to use a lawyer, however. It is easier to conduct your own case if you are defending, for instance, a possession action, than if you are bringing the action, for example for disrepair, but you are more likely to be at risk of losing your home in an action you have to defend than in one you bring to court yourself.

It is not possible in a book of this length to describe how to bring or defend legal proceedings, although in the case of a small claim you will be able to get advice from court officials; and if you are defending an action you will, similarly, get some help, either from court officials or indeed from the judge (part of whose duty it is to ensure that people do not suffer for want of a lawyer).

As a general rule, you should be careful to comply with any instructions which accompany forms from a court or elsewhere (for instance, if a possession claim is issued against you, you ought to indicate within two weeks whether or not you propose to defend, and on what grounds).

You are unlikely, as a litigant in person, to be penalised *in a court*, for non-compliance with such requirements, but you will certainly be better placed if you do comply. If you are homeless (Chapter 1), under the right to buy (Chapter 5), or in relation to appeals from a Rent Officer to a Rent Assessment Committee (Chapter 8), failure to observe time limits could cost you your rights.

Always attend a court at the time and place stated on a court form: there is nothing more disastrous than failure to turn up.

If you *cannot* be present, for example because you are ill, *always* notify the court in advance, and in writing, and if possible send someone along to explain to the judge (not just to a court official). Do *not* leave the explanation until later, when orders against you may have already been made and you then have to try to get them set aside.

Can I get help with legal advice?

In addition to the legal-aid scheme, there is a legal advice scheme which enables a lawyer to administer a rough-and-ready means-test, and give you advice (including letter-writing and filling in forms, but falling short of actually appearing on your behalf before a court), either for free or for a small sum of money. This is particularly useful in relation to the Rent Tribunal or Rent Officer or Assessment Committee, or if you are trying to prosecute a criminal case yourself, when full legal aid is not available.

In addition, there are now several advice and aid agencies which operate either through voluntary or government funding and which as a rule make no charge for their services, which can extend to full representation.

The best known of these are the Citizens' Advice Bureaux which have, over the years, built up a considerable experience in advising tenants. There is likely to be one in or near your area. CABx do not usually undertake representation in court, but can in other forums.

There are also Law Centres, of which the staffs include qualified practising lawyers, who will frequently appear in court, either to defend or to bring a case, and in housing matters either in the civil or the criminal courts. They will also act in other forums.

There may be a Law Centre in your area. They may utilise legal aid (in order to increase the otherwise inadequate funds of these agencies) but will almost never ask for money from you. Always co-operate with their efforts to get you covered by legal aid: they are helping you, and by your co-operation you can help them to help others.

In addition, the majority of local authorities maintain Housing Aid Centres. These have the advantage that, if you are entitled to accommodation from the authority itself, you are in effect "in touch" with it from the outset of your problem; the disadvantage is that, for this same reason, the authority may be more inclined to advise you to defend what is perhaps not a defensible action.

Their other disadvantage is that, if your landlord is the local authority, while it may try and help you to "sort things out" by negotiation or agreement, once it is clear that the landlord is not going to do what you want, you will have to go somewhere else for help, i.e. they cannot "fight themselves".

Housing Aid Centres should be distinguished from Housing Action Centres, which are purely voluntary agencies, and neither employed by nor generally answerable to local authorities. There are also other local advice and action agencies, most of which will help in housing matters.

Finally, there are specialist agencies, only a few of which employ their own practising lawyers, but who will usually be fairly well experienced in housing matters. The central such specialist agency is in London: SHAC, the Housing Aid Centre, 189a Old Brompton Road, London SW5 (telephone: 01-373 7276).

The names of local agencies, or sometimes of solicitors appropriate for this sort of work, can be obtained from the Legal Action Group, 242 Pentonville Road, London N1 9UN (telephone: 01-833 2931), and from Shelter, 157 Waterloo Road, London, SE1 (telephone: 01-633 9377). Shelter maintains local groups covering a number of areas and will be able to tell you if there is a group in your area.

It will always be worthwhile to contact a local advice or aid agency before approaching a solicitor, for the reason stated above: they will be able to put you in touch with lawyers willing to work on legal aid, and possibly with the necessary experience.

Will any government agencies help me?

If you are a housing association tenant, and are dissatisfied with your landlord, you can always complain direct to the Housing Corporation, whose responsibility it is to supervise and "monitor" housing associations. Their address is: Maple House, 149 Tottenham Court Road, London W1 (telephone: 01-387 9466).

In addition, and especially in relation to the right to buy, the Department of the Environment may provide advice or even assistance to you. Their address is: 2 Marsham Street, London SW1 (telephone: 01-212 3434).

Finally, if what you are complaining about is a local authority, whether as your landlord, or as the body responsible for forcing your landlord to carry out repairs (Chapter 10), or as the body which you think ought to be providing you with accommodation (Chapter 1), or *in any other way*, you can complain of maladministration.

To complain of maladministration, you have to try to get one of your local councillors to forward the complaint. If you cannot do so, the local government Ombudsman has the right to take a complaint direct from you. If you are in doubt, the office of the Ombudsman will give you advice on how to proceed. The addresses are: Commission for Local Administration in England, 21 Queen Anne's Gate, London SW1 (telephone: 01-222 5622), and Commission for Local Administration in Wales, Derwen House, Court Road, Bridgend, Mid-Glamorgan, CF31 1BN (telephone: 0656-61325).